Let It All Go! What Are You "Weighting" For?

Dr. Mary Steele-Agee

ISBN 978-1-0980-7974-1 (paperback)
ISBN 978-1-0980-7975-8 (hardcover)
ISBN 978-1-0980-7976-5 (digital)

Copyright © 2021 by Dr. Mary Steele-Agee

All rights reserved. No part of this publication may be reproduced, distributed, or transmitted in any form or by any means, including photocopying, recording, or other electronic or mechanical methods without the prior written permission of the publisher. For permission requests, solicit the publisher via the address below.

Christian Faith Publishing, Inc.
832 Park Avenue
Meadville, PA 16335
www.christianfaithpublishing.com

All scripture references are taken from the King James Version of the Holy Bible unless otherwise noted.

Printed in the United States of America

Wherefore seeing we also are compassed about with so great a cloud of witnesses, let us lay aside every weight, and the sin which doth so easily beset us, and let us run with patience the race that is set before us.
				Hebrews 12:1

To the memory of Mother Walterene Harper, my dear mother, who lived a Spirit-filled life and trained her children by precept and example to do the same. She served God with all her heart, and the simple but powerful words "Keep on praying" was always her greeting or salutation to everyone she knew and met.

Acknowledgments

This book is a labor of love written in consolation to our souls of the passing of our mother who always left you with this salutation, "Keep on praying". She left a legacy to follow by her example of righteous living, the unsearchable riches that are in the power of prayer, the strength a woman finds when spiritually travailing in prayer and intercession through this legacy we are empowered to live life in submission to God's Word.

The journey in writing this book provided a self-examination of the many sins that can weigh one down in their walk with the Lord. Yes, while we are saved, we have sins/weights that need to be put away from us. Remember, Romans 3:23, God's Word declares, "For all have sinned and come short of the Glory of God." This reflective prayer guide will help to identify "weights/sins" that we need to lay aside so we can run this race unfettered as we all seek a closer walk with Him.

This book provides a list of some of the weights that can hinder our growth and maturity in Christ. My mother is no longer in her earthen vessel to point out weights, sins, and hindrances to us. Perhaps, you have someone in your life who does. So, now we continue our journey with mother's still voice asserting God's word; "Pray without ceasing (1 Thes 5:17)" because it is prayer that will see us through! Thank you, Mother Harper, for leaving such a powerful legacy of prayer! It was because of Mother and in memory of her that the God's J.E.W.E.L.S. (Just Everyday Women Eager to Love and Serve) Ministry was birthed. The Lord has placed some special people in my life to help accomplish His will in this ministry and in this season.

Roberta Couch has contributed substantially with words of encouragement, prayers, writing, and editing of this manuscript. She was the "go-to" contact whenever an idea needed further research and development for inclusion in this manuscript. Without her deep love and faithful commitment to the things of God and the power of prayer, this work may not have come to fruition.

Carolyn Thomas has been a calming influence in this journey. Her thoughts and ideas were always precise and to the point. She was a faithful contributor to this work.

Arlene King is multi-talented; she unselfishly shares her knowledge and love for the Lord. Her contributions and comments were always of a supportive nature in this journey.

Jacqueline Fields is an unapologetic teacher of God's Holy Word. She contributed the initial "spark" for this journey. She is a "fire starter." Without her insistence, this work may not have begun.

Ladonna Floyd contributed her incredible editing skills and her "last minute" suggestions and corrections that "righted the course" of intent in many of the passages. She brought a level-headed viewpoint and a sense of reasoning to this project.

A very special thanks to Cleveland Agee, Jr., my husband, pastor, and best friend, for allowing me the many hours needed for writing and reflection. His warm encouragement, unfeigned support, and confidence in me, along with his gentle nudging and prayers, propelled me to bring this book to fruition.

Thanks to God's J.E.W.E.L.S. Women's Ministry which provides an additional platform for further exploration of God's ordinances and doctrines in the word of God. This ministry has assisted in our spiritual journey as we strive to run this race unencumbered.

Contents

Introduction 13

Preface 15

A Strategic Framework: Exchanges from Bondage to
    Spiritual Freedom 17

Lost: I Once was Lost, but Now I'm Found 21

Heaviness: He Ain't Heavy, He Is My Brother! 24

Anxiety: No Worries God Is in Control! 27

Doubt: Don't Worry, Don't Doubt, God Will Work It Out 30

Double-Minded: A Double-Minded Person Is Unstable
    in All His Ways 33

Hopelessness: Who Is the Hope of Glory? Our God,
    Strong and Mighty! 35

Busyness: Taking Care of "Busyness" 38

Greed: Putting Things in the Right Perspective 41

Loneliness: You Are Never Alone 44

Low Self-Esteem: I Am Somebody 48

Bitterness: Bitterness That Takes Root in the Heart
    Grows Deeper 51

Cheating: Your Sins Will Find You Out 54

Low Self-Worth: "God Don't Make Junk!" 57

Depression: Look Up and Live 60

Brokenness: Putting the Pieces Together Again 63

Overbearing: Less of Me, More of Jesus..........................66
Rejection: Rejected of Men..69
Guilt: Not Guilty, Case Dismissed...................................72
Shame: Who Told You That You Were Naked? 76
Grievous: A Sorrowful Spirit..80
High-Minded: Let God Exalt You! 83
Intimidation: Careful, Giants Do Fall! 87
Timid: I Am Not Afraid..90
Sadness: From Sadness to Service....................................94
Poor Communicator: Speak Easy, Speak Clearly............98
Competitive Spirit: A Rivaling Force 101
Bossiness: You're Not the Boss of Me!...........................104
Insecurity: Wrap Yourself in God's Security Blanket ...107
Stress: Encumbered About with Many Things 110
Unfaithful: Can We Count on You? 113
Slothful: Pick Up the Pace 116
Meanness: The Power of Life and Death Lies in the Tongue 119
Overly Committed: Consider the Ant..........................122
Infidelity: From a Promiscuous Past to a Faithful Future 125
Apathy: Transformed from Passive to Passionate 128
Betrayal: For Thirty Pieces of Silver..............................131
Addictions: You Can Run, But You Can't Hide 134
Anger: God's Anger Management Program 137
Jealousy: The Green-Eyed Monster...............................140
Hurt: Sticks and Stones Break Bones, and Words Can Hurt You Too! 143
Unforgiving: Forgive Seventy Times Seven 146

Hatred: A True Disciple Won't Hate Me Because I'm Beautiful 149
Adultery: Go and Sin No More! 153
Lasciviousness: Lasciviousness, What Does It Mean? 156
Fornication: Don't Defile the Temple 159
Grief: When You Just Can't Seem to Get Over It! 162
Condescending: Behind the Smile Lies a Clever but
  Cruel Tongue 165
Possessive: Dominate Your Own Destiny 167
Vengeful: Eye for an Eye, Tooth for a Tooth? No, Lord,
  You Fight My Battles! 170
Judgmental: If You Are the Judge, Where Is Your Robe? 173
Dejection: You Can't Smell the Smoke on My Clothes 175
Fear: "Fear and Dread, Get Out of My Head" 179
An Invitation to Discipleship 183
Conclusion 187

Introduction

The Power of a Prayer Life

Mama said, "Keep on praying." So, I do, first out of obedience to her, and now, from a place of necessity for my spiritual growth in obedience to God. There seems to be a mystery to the power of prayer which makes it incomprehensible to those without knowledge. How can something so full of mystery be so powerful? Our first reaction to prayer may be avoidance, dismissal, or even devaluing its critical importance. Prayer, we think, is a good idea in theory but does it really make a difference? Yes, it does! Praying is an act of faith. Hebrews 11:6 says, "But without faith it is impossible to please God." Prayer is communicating with God. Prayer will convict hearts and lead to confession. Prayer will lead us to salvation. An effective, fervent prayer life will allow us to respond to the cross of Calvary and the shed blood of Jesus Christ in a most humbling way. Prayer will lead us to a faith explosion as we see the miraculous ways that Jesus responds to us. Jeremiah 33:3 says, "Call unto me and I will answer thee and show thee great and mighty things, which thou know not."

A Christian's prayer life evokes the presence of God, and where God is, so is the power of His anointed presence. The Holy Spirit helps us in our prayer life: "Likewise, the Spirit also helpeth our infirmities: for we know not what we should pray for as we ought: but the Spirit itself maketh intercession for us with groanings which cannot be uttered" (Romans 8:26). As we communicate with God, let us be assured that He hears our prayers. Then let us not fail to acknowledge God for the answers He gives us with praise and thanksgivings.

When we are "born-again," we accept Christ into our lives as our Lord and Savior. Our lives are changed, and we are transformed by the renewing of our minds. We become a new creation in Christ Jesus (2 Corinthians 5:17). The spiritual man or nature desires to be more like Him, but, the carnal man still has a sinful nature. It is not God's will for us to sin, but when we do, it is good to know that Jesus Christ is our propitiation. We have an advocate in Him.

When we go to our heavenly Father in prayer asking for forgiveness, Jesus intercedes for us. When we can't find all the words to say, God listens to our hearts. What a joy He will bring to our weary soul! He promises to hear us when we call, and He promises to answer us. It is a joy to serve a God who can hear our feeble cry, and the prayers of a humble heart. He is one who knows all about us and cares so much for all of us. What a mighty God we serve!

It is never too late to pray! 1Samuel 12:23 tells us not praying is a sin. God does not hear a sinner's prayers when he continues in sin, (Psalms 66:18). So, let us repent before the Almighty God, so that our prayers are not hindered. We can lay aside the "weights and sins" and overcome difficulties in our lives by following God's word. As we call on Him for help and guidance in our time of need, any weights/sins will be exposed! It pleases our heavenly Father to see His children being obedient to His word! God invites us to pray. We are taught in James 4:3 to pray in faith, believing God and He will answer us when we do not pray amiss or to fulfill our own lusts. "Let us therefore come boldly unto the throne of Grace that we might obtain mercy and find grace in our time of need" (Hebrews 4:16). So **let it all go!** Cast all your cares on Him! Lord, we are so thankful to you for the peace that you have given to us and the love and joy that surrounds us when we pray. There is indeed power in prayer!

Preface

The Purpose of This Book

Everyone has *weights in* their lives. These weights have come "which doth so easily beset us" (Hebrews 12:1). There are so many of God's people living and existing with hidden bruises, burdens, and bondages. Many are wounded, hurting, or just living in trespasses and sins. Many have wounds as fresh as right now or as old as the adolescent days of yesteryears. Many don't seem to have the strength to overcome predicaments or the power to resist temptations. Many fall under the indulgence and the acts of sin, only to be found living under condemnation.

Now, some people of God have come to a place in their lives to move forward but are met at an impasse. They cannot identify what is hindering their progress in divine dominion and spiritual warfare. Their Christian authority is weak and powerless. They have a form of godliness but deny the power thereof (2 Timothy 3:5). They cannot seem to get free from the secret sins, the pains, and the bondage. Apostle Paul admonished the saints with these words: "We are surrounded by such a cloud of witnesses, let us lay aside every weight, and sin which doth so easily beset us," (Hebrews 12:1).

There is no sin that is common to man that Christ has not already made a way of escape. In the Word of God, there is an answer for your problem!

This book will help to identify personal weights/sins, offer inspiration, and focus prayers to target the hurts in the lives of people who are willing to exchange bondage for freedom. It was written and designed to help us recognize the offences in our lives that hinder us in spiritual growth and progress. The daily readings provide a starting point for further study and insight into God's ordinances to strengthen your relationship with Him. These readings are offered as a tool to use in developing a strong prayer life. The writings will guide and instruct those needing spiritual stability. It will encourage the reader to develop a prayer life about specific "weights" that hold the Christian in a place of stagnation. It will encourage and strengthen the Christian through the Word of God. It will answer the questions of *why* and *how* to "lay aside every weight / sin" that has become a stronghold in the life of the believer.

As a first step, through an act of repenting, use this as a ministering tool; it will give you needed direction and will open the door for your healing. Now, you are on your way to being made whole through God's Word in prayer!

A Strategic Framework: Exchanges from Bondage to Spiritual Freedom

Escape the Bondage and Exchange it for Freedom

Below is a list of *some* "weights/sins" that can hinder our walk with the Lord and it's corresponding Spiritual Exchange, as we all strive to move from bondage to spiritual freedom.

Bondage of Weight/ Sins	Exchange for Spiritual Freedom	Scripture
Addiction	Independence	I Cor. 10:13
Adultery	Faithfulness	Matt: 26:41
Anger	Agreeable	Ephesians 4:26–27
Anxiety	Peace	Matt. 6:34
Apathetic	Caring	I Peter 5:7
Betrayal	Trustworthy	Proverbs 11:13
Bitter	Sweetness	Ephesians 4:31
Bossiness	Diplomacy	I Peter 5:3
Brokenness	Wholeness	Isaiah 41:10
Busyness	Stillness, Subtlety	Psalm 46:10
Cheating	Fairness, integrity, guilelessness	Proverbs 13:5

Competitive Spirit	Easygoing, cooperative	Philippians 2:3
Condescending	Unpretentious, Demure	Ephesians 4:29
Control	Yielding, Submission	Matt. 6:30
Dejection	Contentment, cheeriness	Prov. 11:9
Depression	Mental Stability	Phil. 4:8
Double-minded / Unstable	Stability	James 1:8
Doubt	Belief	Romans 10:9
Envious	Well-meaning, Kindhearted	Prov. 14:30
Fear	Assurance, confidence, courage, trust	II Timothy 1:7
Fornication	Virtue, Chasity	I Cor. 6:19–20
Greed/Selfish	Generosity, altruistic	Heb. 13:5
Grievousness	Joyfulness, Happiness	Prov. 3:13–18
Guilt	Removal of Condemnation, Innocent	Gal. 5:1
Hatred	Love	Prov. 10:12
Heaviness	Light Heartedness, Jubilation	Isa. 61:3
High-minded	Humility	Phil. 2:3–8
Hopelessness	Anticipative, expectant	Psalm 130:5
Hurt	Comforted	Joshua 1:9
Infidelity	Faithfulness, Loyalty	Hebrews 13:4
Insecurity	Confidence	Isa. 40:31
Intimidation	Reassurance, encouraged	I Peter 3:14
Jealousy	Trustworthy, Admiration	Lam. 3:31–36
Judgmental	Undiscriminating, Appreciative, Charitable	Ezekiel 16:42

Lasciviousness	Decency, Chaste	Matt. 6:13
Loneliness	Contentment, belong	Romans 8:38–39
Lost	Found	Luke 15:6–7
Low Self-esteem	Confident	Psalm 3:3
Low Self-worth	Assurance	Psalm 46:1
Lust	Chastity, Chaste, Pure heartedness	Romans 12:1
Lying/ Untruthfulness	Truth	Prov. 6:16–17
Malice	Empathy	Ephesians 4:31–32
Meanness/Nastiness	Friendly/Kindness	Gal. 5:22–23
Overbearing	Modest	II Cor. 5:17
Overly committed	Balance	Psalm 127:1–2
Poor communicator	Articulate, Fluent	Hebrews 4:16
Possessive	Surrendering	James 4:7–8
Pride	Humility	Prov. 6:16–17
Rejection/ Unworthiness	Acceptance	Jer. 3:12b
Sadness	Happiness	Psalm 34:17
Selfish	Giving	Gal. 6:1–10
Self-righteousness	Nonjudgmental	Titus 3:5
Shame	Honor, Respect	Psalm 40:1–3
Short-tempered	Calmness	Psalm 46:10
Slothful	Industrious, Diligent	Romans 12:11
Timid	Boldness	I Samuel 15:17
Unforgiving	Forgiving	Mark 11:25
Vengeful	Merciful, Considerate	Ephesians 2:4–7

Pray with all diligence for the release of these strongholds. Pray that the spiritual exchanges become prevalent in your life by using the scriptures as a starting point. Pray for insight, enlightenment, direction and confidence to stand in the liberty wherein God has made you free! (Galations 5:1).

NOTE: This list of weights/sins with their corresponding spiritual exchanges is by no means intended to represent one that is all-inclusive, but will prompt you to start the thought process of self-reflection and offer a strategic pathway to a deeper prayer life and subsequent deliverance.

Now, Let's get inspired to examine ourselves and Let It All Go! What Are You "Weighting" For?

The Inspirational Readings and corresponding prayers will help you as you seek to make the necessary "spiritual exchanges" for the bondage of the weights and sins that so easily hinder our growth in the Lord.

We will strive to lay aside every weight and sin in exchange for the spiritual freedom that God wants for His children. He desires for us to live a life free from the bondage of sin and to walk in the spirit of holiness.

Ask God to help you identify the Spiritual Exchange for the "weight/sin" that you are releasing to ensure that you receive your deliverance and remain steadfast in the liberty in which God has made you free, then keep on praying!

I Once was Lost, but Now I'm Found

"Fear not, for I am with you; be not dismayed, for I am your God; I will strengthen you, I will help you, I will uphold you with my righteous right hand." Isaiah 41:10 (NKJV)

Weight/Sin: **Lost**
(Lonely, Unloved, Confused, Hopeless)

Inspiration:

Have you ever been lost and couldn't find your way? Being lost brings about so many other emotions, such as confusion, a sense of panic, even an eerie feeling of, "What if I'm not ever found?" I can remember the feelings of hopelessness when I became lost as a child. Growing up, I was a "daddy's girl." I knew that my daddy loved me unconditionally and that love was reciprocated. Oh, yes, I loved my daddy so. I would wait for my daddy to come home each night from work. I would always be met with such kind and encouraging words that were just for me. Even, when I had been naughty, in his loving way, he knew what to do and what to say to make me not feel so guilty. He would help me to smile again. Oh, what unconditional love!

One day, walking home from school, I became distracted following a small kitten into the wooded area behind our school. When I emerged at the other end of the woods, I was on a street that was unfamiliar to me. I was lost! I sat crying and wondering what to do. Before long, I saw something familiar. It was my father's station wagon coming down the street. It was my father coming to rescue me. Oh, can you imagine the relief and joy I felt!

My father hurried to me, scooped me in his arms, and soothed all my fears! Many times, since then, on my journey of life, I have felt that I had surely wandered too far away from God. I have felt lost many times and without hope. Thanks be to God, we have a heavenly Father who loves His children and will never give up on them! He invites us to call on Him, and He promises He will answer, (Jeremiah 33:3). The Bible tells us, "Be strong and courageous and fear not for the Lord thy God, it is He that go with thee" (Deuteronomy 31:6–8). He will never leave us. He will always come to our rescue. Our heavenly Father will hold us in His loving arms. He can bring so much peace and joy into our lives. He gives hope to those who are lost. Like the warmth of a good father, in Jesus and in Him alone, you will find unspeakable joy!

Prayer:

Heavenly Father, in the name of Jesus, I seek your direction and guidance, there are times that I feel so lost and alone. I do not know where I should go or what my next steps should be. Father, you said that you will never leave me nor forsake me. I pray for your guidance as you lead me into all truth and righteousness as I put my trust in you. I serve a God that is bigger than the universe! "The earth is the Lord's, and the fullness thereof. the world, and they that dwell therein" (Psalm 24:1)! I am yours, and you are mine. You are the God of my salvation and the omnipotent One who knows everything about me. You know me and created me for your purpose. Lord, rescue me from this lost, confused, and hopeless feeling. I know that you love me unconditionally. I feel your love and your care. I thank you for giving me new mercies every morning. You already knew that I needed your mercy as I started my day. Strengthen me as I stand on your promise that all my needs are supplied according to your riches in glory. Help me, Lord, to allow you to work in my life for your glory. I put my confidence and trust in you. Give me what I need to grow more like you each day. Lord, help me to walk in your perfect will as I follow Jeremiah 29:11, that says you have good plans for my life with a hope and a prosperous future. Amen.

Daily encouragement /Further scripture study and readings:

Monday: Luke 15:20–29
Tuesday: Psalm 25:16–17
Wednesday: Luke 19:10
Thursday: Psalm 46:1
Friday: Luke 15:94–106
Saturday: Isaiah 41:10–11
Sunday: Deuteronomy 31:8
(also, see fear, anxiety)

He Ain't Heavy, He Is My Brother!

"We then that are strong ought to bear the infirmities of the weak". Romans 15:1

Weight/Sin: **Heaviness**
(Grief, Grieving, Bereavement)

Inspiration:

Sometimes we feel heaviness in spirit, whether it is from our own burdens or bearing someone else's burdens. When you are going through a difficult time, as a Christian, you must remember that God is in control of the length of time and the intensity of the trials. The enemy cannot do more than God permits. We all reach critical times in our lives when circumstances challenge our strength as well as faith and leaves us feeling heavy in spirit. This heaviness may come as a result of any kind of tragedy, toxic friendship, a dead-end job, strained relationships, situations with family or friends, or whatever difficulty life brings to bear. Whatever the challenge, we must see things through the eyes of God. Take the decisive position that God will not put more on you than you are able to bear. You must "trust in the Lord with all thine heart and lean not unto thine own understanding. In all thy ways acknowledge Him and He shall direct thy paths," (Proverbs 3:5–6). Pray that God will strengthen you and preserve you to come out of your trial victoriously. Because you are more than a conqueror, through Christ Jesus, He can lift the heaviness and make you whole again. Psalm 34:17–18 NIV says "When the Righteous cry for help, the Lord hears and delivers them out of all their troubles. The Lord is near to the brokenhearted and saves the crushed in spirit."

Even amid your own pain, be strong and help bear the infirmities of those who are weak. Job, was a servant of the Lord, he suffered greatly; yet, he repented and prayed for his friends. Job 42:10 reveals that, after Job prayed for his friends, the Lord restored his fortunes and gave him twice as much as he had before! Psalm 34:19 states, "Many are the afflictions of the righteous, but the Lord delivereth him out of them all." And, to this, we can say, "To God be the glory for the great things that He has done for us."

Prayer:

Father, I pray in the name of your matchless son, Jesus. I humbly submit to you. I ask that you lift this burden of heaviness and wrap me in a garment of praise. I release this heaviness to receive joy for my mourning! I pray that my countenance be arrayed once again with your glory. While I am in the midst of this trial may your glory be revealed in me! I love you, Lord, with all my heart. You promised that you will not put more on me than I am able to bear. This grievous situation and heavy burden, I give it to you. I rejoice in knowing that you are a burden bearer, a mind regulator, a heart mender, a soul saver, and the "lifter of my head". It is you, God, and you alone who will bring peace to my mind and rescue me from all my troubles. Forgive me of the sins that I have committed, whether sins by omission or commission, as I strive to be more like you. Jesus, you endured the cross for me, for my salvation. The suffering that I may endure will not compare to the glory that is to come.

I thank you, Lord Jesus, that you loved me so much that you gave your life for me. Isaiah 53, expressed so vividly the agony you endured as the suffering servant. You were bruised for my iniquities, wounded for my transgressions, and the chastisement of my peace was laid on you. You suffered mentally and bodily, as the sin of the world was laid upon your shoulders. You did this all, that I may live! I cast all my anxieties on you because you care for me. Jesus, in you,

I find true contentment. Keep me focused on your everlasting love. I invite you Holy Spirit to give me more of God's peace and rest, in Jesus's name. Amen.

Daily encouragement/Further scripture study and readings:

Monday: Isaiah 61:3
Tuesday: James 4:9
Wednesday: Proverbs 10:1, Proverbs 14:13
Thursday: Romans 9:2
Friday: Peter 1:6
Saturday: Proverbs 12:25
Sunday: Philippians 2:27
(also, see brokenhearted, grief)

No Worries God Is in Control!

"Be anxious for nothing, but in everything by prayer and supplication with thanksgiving, let your requests be made known to God."
Philippians 4:6 (NKJV)

Weight/Sin: **Anxiety**
(Nervousness, Worry, Concern)

Inspiration:

Have you heard the saying "Easier said than done"? When God said in Philippians 4:6, "Be anxious for nothing," God was clear in directing His children not to worry about anything. He and He alone will supply all our needs according to His riches in glory. Sometimes, we find ourselves worrying over the most minuscule things. We must consciously remind ourselves that God will always provide, no matter the circumstances. It is easy to say, I will not worry, but when troubles come if we are not careful, we will fret and seek out answers in all the wrong places instead of looking to God! The Lord already knows what we need. Release all your burdens, worries, and anxieties to Him, today. He is a burden bearer. We must learn what His word teaches: "Count it all joy, when you fall into various temptations," (James 1:2). We should look to the Lord when we face temptations and difficulties that may cause us to worry. Speak the words written in 1 Peter 1:6 over our lives: "In this you greatly rejoice, though now for a little while you may have had to suffer grief in all kinds of trials" (NIV). He knows all about our troubles, nothing is hidden from Him (Hebrews 4:13). Let us not be like the world who resort to other means to pacify themselves. They resort to smoking to calm their nerves. They take up drinking alcohol, drugs, lust violence, promiscuous sexuality, lashing out in anger, or the acquisition of material things—all in attempts to find peace. When anxiety tries to invade, cast it out of your life! Choose to keep your mind on Jesus. He will keep you in perfect peace and be determined to rejoice in the Lord always!

So, be truly glad there is wonderful joy ahead, even though you must endure many trials for a little while. These trials will show that your faith is genuine (I Peter 1:6–7). When we seek Him, instead of it being "easier said", we can count it "done"! God *is* in Control!

Prayer:

Heavenly Father, I acknowledge you for who you are. You are Jehovah Jireh, the one who provides for me! Your word tells us not to worry about the meager things in our lives. We should not worry about what we will eat or drink or what to wear. Our lives are so much more than those things. We see how you take care of the fowls of the air and how you clothed the grass of the field. The evidence of your blessings is everywhere! I see how beautiful the lilies grow without us attending them. Yet, God, you remind us that we are so much more valuable than they. Thank you, God, for caring so much for me and reassuring me that you will take care of all my needs. The only thing that you require of me is that I trust and obey your Word. Lord, give me the heart and fortitude to endure what I'm going through, for I know that happy are those who suffer in your name. I won't worry about the doctor's report because you sent your Word to heal me and deliver me out of all my troubles. I stand on your promises, my heavenly Father. Your promises are yea and Amen.

God, all that you have said in your Word must be accomplished! Your Word will not return unto you void. So, I am settled in faith believing your Word. I release all my cares to you. I will lie down at night with sweet rest, and I will sleep in peace knowing that you care for me. Bless my family and keep them in all their ways. Dispatch ministering angels to abide by our side and keep us safe. When the enemy comes at us one way, your angels will cause them to flee from us in seven different ways! The devil has no dominion over me or my family. We put our trust and confidence in you. We acknowledge you in all our ways and pray that you will continue to direct our paths today, tomorrow, and always. These petitions we lay at your feet, in Jesus' name! Amen.

Daily encouragement /Further scripture study and readings:

Monday: Genesis 4:9
Tuesday: Psalm 25:16–17
Wednesday: Luke 19:10
Thursday: Psalm 46:1
Friday: Luke 15:4–6
Saturday: Isaiah 41: 10–11
Sunday: Deuteronomy 31:8

Don't Worry, Don't Doubt, God Will Work It Out

"Come to me all you who are weary and burdened, and I will give you rest." Matthew 11:28 (NIV)

Weight/Sin: **Doubt**
(Hesitation, Disbelief, Uncertainty)

Inspiration:

Many times, I have felt so overwhelmed by the cares and stresses of this life. At a point in my career, I was appointed to the highest position of the school district in my hometown. Now, I realize that God had prepared me, many years prior, for such an awesome responsibility. However, there were occurrences when I felt that, perhaps, I had taken on more than even I could bear. As the leader, everyone looks to you for answers and solutions to the many problems inherent in a large corporation. With the oversight of over three thousand employees, the task, at times, was quite daunting. I am grateful that I had a personal relationship with God, and I quickly found out just how much I needed Him! I was clear that God had given me the promotion (Psalm 75:6), and I came to know that in difficult times He would sustain me.

I recall one evening, after working long hours, I was troubled and began to doubt God's direction of my career and my life. In the early morning hours, around 3:00 a.m., God awakened me out of my slumber, and very distinctly, I heard His word in Romans 4:20–21, "He staggered not at the promise of God through unbelief; but was strong in faith, giving glory to God; And being fully persuaded that, what He had promised, He was able also to perform." I was reassured by my God that He will see me through and with good success.

I am now retired and enjoying the blessings of the Lord. Looking back, I can easily see that those times were sent my way to test and build my faith in God. The enemy wants to use doubt and stress as forms of distractions to derail us and to get us off course. The devil is a liar and the father of all lies! (John 8:44). My God will never put more on us than we are able to bear. He will see us through all our difficult moments. I am reminded of His word in Psalms 34:19 that says: "Many are the afflictions of the righteous, but the Lord delivereth him out of them all." "With man it is impossible, but not with God. For all things are possible with God," (Mark 10:27, ESV). And Romans 8:28 reminds us that God is working things out to our benefit. "All things work together for good to them that love God, to them who are the called according to His purpose."

You too may have some doubts of God's blessings in your life. You may have questioned, "Why am I going through difficulties in this season of my life?" I have learned: if God said it, then, believe it! That you may live a life of faith and never be in doubt of His Word. Don't worry, don't doubt because God will work it out for you. Then you can say, unequivocally, "to God be the Glory, for the things that he has done!"

Prayer:

Father, in the name of your precious son, Jesus who shed his blood for our redemption; I thank you for all that you have done and continue to do in my life. Even when it appears that my petitions are unnoticed, I know that you hear me and will answer me. Lord, I need your help in the area of doubt. I ask for direction and guidance that will help me rely wholly on you. I need you to operate fully in my life. Give me, Lord what I lack, equip me for your purposes, help me go beyond my present circumstances and take me into the glorious future you have preordained for me. I know the plans that you have for me are good. Help me to remove all fear, doubt, and discontentment. Help me to lay aside every weight and all sins that so easily hold me back from running this race with patience, endurance, and grace. Lord, breathe life into my dreams and my aspirations, breathe new life into my relationships that I may love others as you love me. Lord, help me do things your way, that your will be done in my life.

I confess that I can do all things through Christ who will give me the strength to complete, with excellency and precision, the tasks that lie ahead. Help me to not settle for the less or mundane in my life. There is a more excellent way of living. I choose to live according to your Word. Father, as I draw nearer to you and obey your commands, you will draw nearer to me. Forgive me of my trespasses as I forgive those who trespassed against me. Your way, not my way, is the key to living a victorious life. Amen.

Daily encouragement /Further scripture study and readings:

Monday: Matthew 19:26
Tuesday: Matthew 14:3
Wednesday: James 1:5–8
Thursday: John 20:24–29
Friday: 1 Corinthians 5:7
Saturday: Genesis 17:15–21, 18:10–14
Sunday: Acts 1:3–4, 14:15–18

A Double-Minded Person Is Unstable in All His Ways

"Draw near to God and He will draw near to you. Cleanse your hands, you sinners, and purify your hearts, you double-minded." James 4:8 (ESV)

Weight/Sin: **Double-minded**
(Irresolute, Inconclusive, Vacillating)

Inspiration:

Do you find it challenging to make up your mind at times? Is it hard for you to make a decision and stick to it? Are you indecisive? Do you *straddle the fence* when it comes to making a choice? If your answer to any of these questions is "yes", then there is a need for a clearer focus on your thoughts and actions. We need to seek God for clarity in our decision-making. The Bible tells us that "a double-minded man is unstable in all his ways" (James 1: 8). God recognized the double-minded when Elijah confronted the people of Israel by asking: "How long will you waver between two opinions? If the Lord is God, follow Him; but if Baal is god, follow him" (1 Kings 18:21). God wants us to be decisive in our walk and in our relationship with Him. We must choose with determination and clarity whom we will serve! When we make God our savior, let us strive to have His mind, His thoughts, and His character. Paul wrote in Philippians 2:5, "Let this mind be in you, which was also in Christ Jesus." When we have the mind of Christ, we will allow the Holy Spirit to guide us, and our actions will be in line with His word. "The

Lord is near to all who call upon Him, to all who call upon Him in truth". As children we learn to make decisions based on what we are taught from our parents, teachers in Sunday school, grade school and others that had some significance in our upbringing. We learn early to make choices and experience the consequences of our good or bad selections. Let us learn to trust God and not be double-minded. Trusting will help us live a stable life as we put our confidence in Him. We can experience His goodness. Choosing God is easy when we fully understand who He really is!

Prayer:

Heavenly Father, in the name of Jesus, I thank you that you are all that I ever need! In you, I lack nothing. Today, I pray for a closer walk with you. I pray for clarity in my thoughts, as I seek a God-sanctioned purpose for my life, as is promised in Jeremiah 29:11. You said in your Word, you will keep them in perfect peace whose mind is stayed on you. I seek peace in making decisions that will govern my life. Help me base my decisions according to your Word, that I may never doubt or waver in the knowledge of the plans that you have for me. I pray that my decisions won't have a negative impact on others. And, that I am daily growing in your grace as I obtain mercy in all my doings. Lord, help me to see the road ahead clearly. Your Word is a lamp unto my feet and a light unto my pathway that will guide me in the direction of the cross. Lord, I will forever thank you for your guidance, leading me into all that is truth. Amen.

Daily encouragement /Further scripture study and readings:

Monday: James 1:8
Tuesday: 2 Kings 18:21
Wednesday Psalm 119:113–115
Thursday: Isaiah 29:13
Friday: Matthew 23:25–28
Saturday: Luke 11:39–40
Sunday: Matthew 6:24

Who Is the Hope of Glory? Our God, Strong and Mighty!

"Why are you cast down, O my soul, and why are you in turmoil within me? Hope in God; for I shall again praise him, my salvation and my God." Psalm 42:11 (ESV)

Weight/Sin: **Hopelessness**
(Despair, Uselessness, Impossibilities)

Inspiration:

Hope is a fundamental part of the Christian faith. Our hope in God grows through communing with Him in prayer and encountering Him through His Word. If you feel a sense of hopelessness know that it is not of God. The enemy desires to "sift us like wheat." He wants to deplete everything that is good in our lives. This hope that we speak of is not found in horoscopes, tea leaves, tarot cards, soothsayers, wishbones, false prophets, or wishful thinking. It is none of those worldly things. They are distractions from the truth. Hope is the confident expectations of good things to come. Hebrews 6:11 calls our faith "the full assurance of hope." The Word of God warns us that Satan comes to "steal, kill, and to destroy." He comes to steal your dreams and dash your hope! But, Jesus says, "I have come that they may have life, and that they may have it more abundantly!" (John 10:10, NKJV). You can have that blessed hope in Jesus Christ. You can allow your life to be transformed by the renewing of your mind, by reading and meditating on the scripture's day and night.

Remember, 2 Corinthians 5:7 says, "We walk by faith, not by sight." Our faith, our hope is built on the finished work of Jesus Christ and the promises found in God's Word. None of God's promises in the Bible will ever fail. Joshua 21:45 reads, "There failed not one of any good thing which the Lord had spoken unto the house of Israel, all came to pass." As Christians, we are confident that, God "is able to do exceedingly abundantly above all that we ask or think, according to the power that work in us" Ephesians 3:20 (NKJV). Blessed be the God and Father of our Lord Jesus Christ who has blessed us with every spiritual blessing in the heavenly places in Christ: Just as He chose us in Him before the foundations of the world, that we should be holy and blameless before Him. In love He predestined us to adoption as sons through Jesus Christ Himself, according to the kind intention of His will, to the praise of the glory of His grace, which He freely bestowed on us, His beloved (paraphrase of Ephesians 1:3–6). Let us "rejoice in hope, be patient in tribulation and continue to be instant in prayer" Romans 12:12 (NKJV).

Prayer:

Heavenly Father, Our God strong and mighty! Help me, sustain me, and don't let the enemy triumph over me! Lord I ask you to have mercy on me. Build me up where I have fallen short according to your Word. I am not one without hope because my life is hidden in you. I reject Satan's attempt to bring hopelessness to my thoughts and actions. God, you are a merciful God. I ask that you refresh me with your presence and solidify my hope in you as you bring clarity to my purpose of life. Propel forth my dreams in you, Lord, because you promise in your Word, you will give me good success. The Word says, "When the righteous cry for help, the Lord hears and delivers them out of all their troubles." Hear my prayer, Oh Lord, and send your deliverance, in Jesus' name. Amen.

Daily encouragement / Further scripture study and readings:

Monday: 1 Peter 1:3, 23
Tuesday: Romans 15:4
Wednesday: Romans 5:5
Thursday: Titus 2:11–14
Friday: Psalm 33:20–22
Saturday: Psalm 43:5
Sunday: Matthew 11:28

Taking Care of "Busyness"

"Be still and know that I am God." Psalm 46:10

Weight/Sin: **Busyness**
(Overloaded, Buried, Swamped)

Inspiration:

All kinds of things can interrupt our quiet time, such as: the busyness of everyday living, career responsibilities, raising our children, household chores, traffic jams, telephone calls, text messages, relationships, waiting in line at the grocery store, gas stations, etc., the list can go on and on. The Holy Bible places a high value on peaceful living, calmness, and finding time to rest. Jesus had to escape from the crowds, on many occasions during His ministry, to rest and renew His strength. As Christians, it is easy for us to get caught up in this fast-paced society. This world is full of instantaneous and postmodern occurrences where everything is at our fingertips in a moment. There are twenty-four hours in a day. That's 1,440 minutes or 86,400 seconds. That sure seems like a lot of time to get things done. Often, we rush into our day, and at the day's end, there were just not enough hours to do all the things in which we found ourselves involved.

We can be better situated if we remember what the Word of God says in Psalm 46:10, "Be still and know that I am God." We are reminded to learn to be still so that we can "hear" from God and be ready to do what God wants us to do. Proverbs 3:5–6 says, "Trust in the Lord with all thine heart and lean not unto thine own understanding. In all thy ways acknowledge Him and He shall direct thy paths." In our acknowledging God, He promises to direct us in the ways that we should go. "For I know the plans I have for you, declares the Lord. Plans to prosper you and not to harm you, plans to give you a hope and a future." (Jeremiah 29:11, NIV). God has great plans for you and me. According to his Word, we see that God holds the future for our lives because our lives are designed by Him. How wonderful to know that our lives are already planned out by God! When we acknowledge Him, consult with Him, and ask Him for our daily direction, our lives will take on more meaning, a sense of knowing how to regulate a schedule and prioritize our day.

When we pray and ask God to direct us and help us to shake off the "busyness" of our minds, (with the thoughts of the day swirling around in our heads), He will grant us an unspeakable calmness. He will give us a "peace that surpasses all understanding." We can rest assured knowing that He is in control of all that occurs in our day. A feeling of accomplishment will follow at the end of the day when we put God first. God will always steer us in the right direction.

Prayer:

Father, in the name of Jesus, help me to remember as I read your Holy Word that I am in your presence. Lord, teach me, lead me, guide me, as I take your yoke upon me to learn of your ways and precepts. Create in me a clean heart and renew a right spirit within me. I ask you to still my mind, so I can learn more about your unfettered love for me. Father, I ask that you build me up where I am torn down. Keep me in the center of your will as I learn to wait in my stillness for an answer from you. Help me not to be quick to move on my own, that my steps may be ordered by you. Lord, teach me how to relax and rest in your presence. Your Word reminds me to "stand still and see the salvation of the Lord." So, I seek your guidance as I start this day. Help me to prioritize my activities, always putting you first in all that I do, and never failing to thank you for new mercies every morning. Amen.

Daily encouragement / Further scripture study and readings:

Monday: Psalm 46:10
Tuesday: Thessalonians 3:11–14
Wednesday: Luke 10:38–42
Thursday: Psalm 143: 7–8
Friday: Matthew 6:33
Saturday: Proverbs 3:5–6
Sunday: Ephesians 5:15–17

Putting Things in the Right Perspective

"One gives freely, yet grows all the richer, another withholds what he should give, and only suffers want." Proverbs 11:24 (ESV)

Weight/Sin: **Greed, Selfishness**
(Overconsumption, Hoarding, Covetousness)

Inspiration:

"Do not love the world or the things in the world. If anyone loves the world, the love of the Father is not in him. For all that is in the world, the lust of the flesh, the lust of the eyes, and the pride of life, is not from the Father but is from the world. The world is passing away along with its lusts, but he who does the will of God abides forever" (1 John 2:15–17, NKJV). How many of us have accumulated so many material things over our lifetime, things we do not use anymore, but still hang on to them? None of these "things" can we take with us at our journey's end. We spend our lives seeking after more. We want the latest, biggest, best, and fastest things on the market. There is a point of excessiveness! Our society recurrently introduces the new and improved, the mega and the supersized, the greatest and the fastest which with time will become obsolete.

The knowledge of man is steadily evolving. He will continue to manufacture goods that will prove to be the smallest, biggest, best, and fastest to appeal to the consumer; and we get them whether we can afford it or not. All of these "adjectives" call out for us to increase our assets, possessions and have ownership of more natural and material things. We all seem to want the latest gadget, ones that claim to make life easier. Be aware, that the newest devices always promise to be better in some way or faster to save time, even temptingly shinier and more appealing.

What is it about us that desire the "latest" trend? I know that "things" can "weigh" us down. They can become a weight to our spiritual growth. When we allow the pursuit of "things" to overtake us and occupy our time and deplete our energy, so much so that there is no time left to seek and serve the Lord as we ought, then it is a weight. When we allow "things" to become a distraction, other important aspects of our lives will go lacking. It will serve us well to remember and put into our daily practice, the words in Matthew 6:33, "Seek ye first the kingdom of God and His righteousness and all these things shall be added unto you." God's word also says, in 3 John 2, "I wish above all things that thou mayest prosper and be in health even as thy soul prospereth." Please don't misunderstand, God wants to bless us. He wants us to enjoy and have some of the finer things in life. Greed and selfishness are not behaviors that are practiced in the kingdom of God. We need to lay aside the weight and sin of greed and put our hearts and assets in its right perspective. Nothing should overshadow our obedience and take away from our walk with Him!

In Christianity, it is considered a sin if the excessive desire for "things" will cause us to withhold from the needy. Especially, when we get caught up in overindulging that we forget about others. Simply put, "But whosoever has this world's good and seeth his brother have need, and shut up his bowels of compassion from him, how dwelleth the love of God in him?" (1 John 3:17).

Prayer:

Eternal Father, in your precious son's name, Jesus, I come to you, thanking you for all your blessings and benefits extended to me. You are a gracious God! I declare that I am blessed because I fear you and delight in obeying your commands. According to your Word, as

I am willing and obedient, I will eat the good of the land. Material things are convenient and nice to have, but I don't want things to overshadow my relationship with you. Ecclesiastes 7:12 says, "For wisdom is a defense and money is a defense: but the excellency of knowledge is that wisdom giveth life to them that have it." I am reminded that wisdom and money can get almost everything, but only wisdom can save my life. Lord, I choose life, life in you! I desire wisdom to follow your will for my life. Help me to use your blessings entrusted to me to bless others. Help me to discern the needs of others and be a resource as you lead me. I pray that as my resources increase, I am not only a help to the body of Christ, but others as well. Lord, I stand in agreement with your Word concerning my finances, my prosperity, and my service in your kingdom. Lord, I realize that it is you alone, who has blessed me! I thank you for giving me the ability to obtain the things that I need. Lord, help me to resist the temptation to pile up material things here on this earth, but rather, lay my treasures up in heaven where rust and moth will not corrupt them. I seek first your Kingdom and your righteousness in my life, and you will make sure I have everything that I need. I will follow you in all aspects of my life, including my finances. Amen.

Daily encouragement/Further scripture study and readings:

Monday: Luke12:15
Tuesday: I John 2:16
Wednesday: 2 Corinthians 9:7
Thursday: Ecclesiastes 5:10
Friday: Hebrews 13:5
Saturday: Luke 12:15
Sunday: Matthew 6:24

You Are Never Alone

"For He hath said I will never leave thee nor forsake thee." Hebrews 13:5

Weight/Sin: **Loneliness**
(Solitude, Isolation, Alienation)

Inspiration:

Loneliness is a feeling of isolation or a state of being without companionship. If you struggle with loneliness, then you are certainly not alone. I came to an understanding that many people struggle with loneness. Loneliness sets in when people find themselves alone or alienated. The elderly are not the only people who suffer with the feelings of being lonely. It can be found among children, teenagers, and young adults as well. The consequence of being neglected, shunned, mistreated, and friendless can result in feeling abandoned, isolated, alienated, and lonely. The same holds true for the elderly, as they grow older, their spouses, relatives, and close friends pass away. They lose their companions. They find themselves living alone. They come to feel isolated and alienated as well. They spend their days alone, unlike the life they once knew.

In a world that changes from moment to moment, uncertainties abound! We unfriend, unlike, and unfollow others when we no longer want a relationship or any involvement with them. What if Jesus grows tired of us? He does not change! Jesus Christ is the same yesterday, today, and forever (Hebrews 13:8). "Therefore, as God's chosen people, holy and dearly loved, clothe yourselves with compassion, kindness, humility, gentleness and patience. Bear with each other and forgive one another if any of you have a grievance against someone. Forgive as the Lord forgave you. "And above all these virtues put on love, which binds them all together in perfect unity" (Colossians 3:14, NIV). We are assured from God's Word that He will love us and will always desire a closer relationship with us. He calls us to love each other, even our enemies (Matthew 5:43). "A new commandment I give unto you, that ye love one another; as I have loved you, that ye also love one another" (John 13:34). He loves us with an everlasting love! Could we trust God to remain the same? Yes, His Word says, "For I am the Lord, I change not" (Malachi 3:6). In Christ, you are never alone.

No matter the age, gender, or relationship status, we all need fellowship and companionship to thrive. In Jesus Christ, you can find divine companionship. He is the one who will comfort you. He is a friend that sticks closer than a brother (Proverbs 18:24). Loneliness can become a weight if you give in to it. Satan will cause you to feel empty and as if there is no hope. He tries to convince you to fill that void with things or actions that will lead to destruction. The Bible says that "Satan comes to kill, steal and destroy; but Jesus comes so that we might have life in its fullest measure" (John 10:10). The weight of loneliness can be overcome simply by recognizing the truth of God's presence is continually with you. Start by realizing that it is a lie from Satan that you are lonely. God has promised that He will never leave you nor forsake you.

When you accepted salvation, you received all the promises of God. Now, you must take God at His Word. "Submit thy ways unto the Lord, resist the devil and he will flee from you" (James 4:7). Learn to fight against loneliness by guarding your heart and mind. You must be careful of what you feed your mind and spirit. If you are not careful, you may find yourself seeking companionship in all the wrong places. Stop turning to the Internet, social media, or ungodly gatherings seeking companionship. You may need to stop watching romantic movies if they make you feel lonely. If you are divorced, widowed, an empty nester, or alone for any reason. Learn to plan for holidays, birthdays, and special occasions so that you will be in the company of friends and loved ones. Above all, stop thinking of yourself and turn your focus toward God. Spend more time with Him through meditation, reading, studying, and memorizing the Word. When you spend the time with the Lord, He will fill any void in your life. He promises to "supply all your needs according to his riches in glory" (Philippians 4:19), *even* for companionship. As we experience His grace, He will let us know that we are never alone.

Prayer:

Precious Father, thank you for giving me grace and courage to stand even when I find myself overcome with the weight of loneliness. I know you are concerned about those things that concern me. Help me never to become discouraged or depressed so much that I fail to realize that you are with me always. You have assured me in your Word that you will never leave me nor forsake me. Help me, Father, to embrace those words and believe your promise. God, it is not your will that we live our lives in isolation. You want us to enjoy companionship. We desire companionship that is true, pure, and godly. Help us to be a true, pure, and godly companion to others in our relationships with them.

Keep our hearts and minds right before you as we show ourselves friendly to others. Give us understanding, discernment, and wisdom in choosing companionship. Lead us into the pathway of truth and protect us from the influences of the evil one. Allow into our lives the right companions, the ones that you choose for us as we seek to do your will for our lives. I ask you, God, to lift the weight of loneliness and help me find sweet communication with you through your Holy Spirit. I will rejoice in your presence in my life. I ask that you send godly persons into my life for friendship as my relationship is strengthen with you. I ask in the name of Jesus. Amen.

Daily encouragement/Further scripture study and readings:

Monday: Psalm 27:10
Tuesday: 1 Samuel 12:22
Wednesday: Psalm 25:16

LET IT ALL GO! WHAT ARE YOU "WEIGHTING" FOR?

Thursday: Matthew 28:20
Friday: Romans 8:31–38
Saturday: Psalm 68:5–6
Sunday: Deuteronomy 31:6

I Am Somebody

"Blessed be the Lord thy God, which delighted in thee." 1 Kings 10:9

Weight/Sin: **Low Self-Esteem**
(Lacking Pride, Unappreciated, Inadequacy)

Inspiration:

Self-esteem is having a sense of self-acceptance. It is liking and respecting yourself. How well you like yourself is influenced by several things. Your self-esteem may be at a high level or a low level. Low self-esteem can be attributed to negative treatment, unkind things spoken to you and about you, childhood abuse, or a lack of motivation.

Mostly every one of us will experience some feelings of inadequacy or suffer from low self-esteem sometime in our lives. Perhaps we heard words spoken to us like "That's not enough!" "That's too little!" "You're not good enough!" "What? Are you stupid!?" Every time these words or the like are spoken in malice, it is like peeling wallpaper off the walls of one's character, exposing the bare soul. "You're too dumb! Let someone else do that." "You can't seem to do anything right!" Statements like these have emotional consequences that damages a person's spirit. Degrading words can slowly tear down and strip a person's pride and their self-worth (see the weight on Self-Worth). It will leave a person to question their abilities, feel inadequate, and question their proficiencies. Having low self-esteem will cause one to narrowly focus only on the things that are lacking. They may lose their confidence, and in severe cases, they even lose their self-respect! What is keeping you from liking and respecting yourself? If it is past sins, then know that no matter how terrible the sin, God has forgiven you, so you can forgive yourself. There is no need to feel any condemnation because you belong to Jesus Christ, (Romans 8:1). Whenever these thoughts come to mind, we can replace them with thoughts reminding ourselves how God sees us. He sees us as worthy, so much that He gave His only begotten Son to save us!

If you are experiencing feelings of condemnation and self-loathing, then know that it is not coming from God. He loves and cares for you. Knowing who you are is strongly related to your self-esteem. It is so important to know who you are in Christ and what the Word of God says about who you are. Do not allow others to define you with unkind and negative words. Define yourself through the Word of God. I am who God says I am! "I am fearfully and wonderfully made" (Psalm 139:14). God's works are wonderful, and His workmanship is marvelous! Why harbor feelings of low self-esteem when the Bible, in Romans 8:17, tells us that we are heirs of God and a joint heir with Christ? Romans 8:37 defines you as more than a conqueror. No weight or sin and no attempt of Satan can steal the loving care of God from us, and that makes us more than conquerors through Christ who loves us. We are not only victorious; we are overwhelmingly victorious! Begin today to confess out of your mouth what God, through His word, says about you. Now take your rightful place. You are somebody in Christ Jesus. You are a child of the King!

Prayer:

Lord God, your grace is sufficient for me! Your power is made perfect in weakness. Father, I come boldly before your throne of grace seeking help and mercy. Lord, I confess before you my shortcomings and confess your Word concerning me. I ask that you heal me of every cause of my low self-esteem. Help me to speak positive things to myself according to your Word. Help me to see myself as you see me. I rejoice that I am your child and that you love me. You commanded me to be strong and courageous. You told me not to be afraid or discouraged, for you are always with me wherever I may go. Lord, remind me of this truth whenever I feel disheartened about my inability to accomplish the tasks set before me or hear the murmurings of others putting me down. Lord, I lay aside this weight of low esteem to become the person you would have me to be. I bless you, God, that you are showing me how to love myself as I love you more. These things I pray in Jesus' name. Amen.

Daily encouragement/Further scripture study and readings:

Monday: 1 Samuel 16:7
Tuesday: 1 John 4:10
Wednesday: 2 Peter 5:7
Thursday: Psalm 139:13–14
Friday: Song of Solomon 4:7
Saturday: Isaiah 49:16
Sunday: 1 Peter 2:9
(Also see self-worth)

Bitterness That Takes Root in the Heart Grows Deeper

> "Let all bitterness, and wrath, and anger, and clamor, and evil speaking be put away from you, with all malice: And be ye kind one to another, tenderhearted, forgiving one another, even as God for Christ's sake hath forgiven you."
> Ephesians 4:31–32

Weight/Sin: **Bitterness**
(Harshness, Hostility, Hatred, Deep-seated ill will)

Inspiration:

Life can be so hard and not always by your own hand. Then, at times, life seems so unfair. It is like the world has passed out to everyone a bowl of cherries, and all you got are the pits! It can become so discouraging to the point that it'll affect your outlook on life. We have all experienced disappointments at one time or another. If you haven't, you will sooner or later. When disappointment comes, beware of the tactics of Satan. He will, with all subtlety, cause that disappointment to turn to resentment and root into bitterness. How do we counteract this? By safeguarding our heart and learning how to forgive. Ephesians 4:31–32 admonishes us to get rid of bitterness by forgiving one another; let it all go and stop holding grudges. Ask God to forgive you of your trespasses as you forgive those who trespass against you! Don't allow bitterness to take root in your heart. It is like a seed planted that takes root, and that small root grows deeper and has the probability to produce a large tree. Bitterness that takes root in the heart has the potential to produce the fruit of jealousy, dissension, and possibly even greater sins. The root and the fruit of bitterness is all sin before God because he called us to love one another as He has loved us. When disappointment comes, what will you do with the pain? Give it to God! Yes, people will hurt you, mistreat you, and despitefully use you, but the child of God is warned to forgive and forget (see the weight on Unforgiving). The Bible, in Luke 6:28, tells us to bless those who curse us, to love our enemies and pray for them who despitefully use us. When we are obedient to the Word of God, then God will lift our heavy burdens! When life gives you lemons, make lemonade and share the sweet treat with others. When life gives you cherry pits, plant the seeds; soon you'll reap a harvest of cherries!

Don't take afflictions and disappointments to heart and allow Satan to torment you personally, for God said in His Word, "Many are the afflictions of the righteous, but God delivereth him out of them all" Psalm 34:19. He alone can heal the hurt that causes bitterness.

Prayer:

Dear God, I come before your throne of grace. There were times that I did not forgive those who trespassed against me. I ask for your forgiveness. I repent now, God, for allowing bitterness to enter in. I submit it to you and trust you to heal me in this area. Remove the very root of it from my heart. Lord, I pray for my enemies that their hearts are softened and that you heal the hurt in their lives, and they no longer seek to harm me. I thank you, Lord, and praise you for lifting this weight from me that I might run this race with patience, in Jesus' name. Amen.

Daily encouragement/Further scripture study and readings:

Monday: Hebrews 12:15
Tuesday: James 3:14

LET IT ALL GO! WHAT ARE YOU "WEIGHTING" FOR?

Wednesday: Ephesians 4:31–32
Thursday: Mark 11:25
Friday: Isaiah 38:1
Saturday: Leviticus 19:18
Sunday: Proverbs 16:32
(see weight, unforgiveness, jealousy, hurt)

Your Sins Will Find You Out

"Blessed is the man unto whom the Lord imputeth not iniquity, and in whose spirit, there is no guile". Psalm 32:2

Weight/Sin: **Cheating**
(Deceitful, Dishonest, Fraud, Guile)

Inspiration:

The world offers us easy ways to "put one over" on other people, be deceptive, not owning our mistakes, and how to slip out of hard situations leaving someone else holding the bag! Our society has ready-made answers that are not always legitimate, and they call it the way of life. There are temptations all around us to cheat and be deceitful. When we are temped, it is an opportunity for us to make a choice to be honest or dishonest. Yes, we all have temptations! When we act on them and the deed is done, then it is sin. What is cheating? It is deception, trickery, craftiness, cunningness, misinformation, untruth, and guile. If you found an adjective in this list that describes your behavior, then you have a deceitful heart, and you are a cheater! This means that you will manipulate the truth in order to take advantage of a person or situation. God has specific requirements as to how we are to conduct ourselves and treat each other.

We cannot allow deceit to enter our spirit. Christ is our perfect example. "Because Christ also suffered for us, leaving us an example, that we should follow his steps: Who did no sin, neither was guile found in his mouth" (1Peter 2:21–22). Cheating is a characteristic of the old nature. Before salvation, we lied or cheated to get out of trouble, but now we can trust Christ because He is a present help in the time of trouble. 2 Peter 1:4 lets us know that we can partake of God's divine nature. He empowers us to put on the new man, which, after God, is created in righteousness and true holiness. Are you a person who is dishonest in your marriage or relationships? Perhaps, you are that person who withheld information on tax forms to ensure a larger refund. Do you dislike losing so much, that you will be deceitful in order to win? Maybe, you are less than honest in your business transactions. Whatever the case may be, if it is dishonest and an attempt to be deceptive for your own benefit, you can stop and make a change. The weight of cheating will be lifted when you take it to the Lord in earnest, sincere prayer and seek His forgiveness. Make an exchange from a life of cheating to a truthful and faithful life in Christ. Make every effort to be completely honest in all that you do. Remember, nothing is hidden from God. "The eyes of the Lord are in every place beholding the evil and the good" (Proverbs 15:3). Be careful to be honest in all your dealings because, you may escape judgment for a season, but "your sins will find you out"! (Numbers 32:23).

Prayer:

Dear Father, in the name of Jesus, I ask that you help me to be honest always. I realize that nothing is hidden from you. I seek your forgiveness; my life is naked and open before you, and you know my ways. Lord, I'm giving this deceitful heart to you, once and for all, asking that you create in me a clean heart and renew the right spirit in me. Your love overwhelms me. I praise you for the comfort I have in the Holy Spirit. Thank you for taking this weight from me and giving me your peace. In the name of Jesus, I pray. Amen.

Daily encouragement /Further scripture study and readings:

Monday: Psalm 34:13
Tuesday: 2 Peter 3:10
Wednesday: Jeremiah 17:9–10
Thursday: Proverbs 24:28

DR. MARY STEELE-AGEE

Friday: Proverbs 19:1
Saturday: 2 Corinthians 1:12
Sunday: James 4:17

"God Don't Make Junk!"

"I will praise thee for I am fearfully and wonderfully made marvelous are thy works; and that my soul knoweth right well." Psalm 139:14

Weight/Sin: **Low Self-Worth**
(Devalued, Low-Regard, Low Pride)

Inspiration:

How do you value yourself? Have you come to see yourself as God sees you? Or, have you allowed unhealthy thoughts and feelings to take you into the bondage of low self-worth? If so, it is time for you to replace your thoughts with God's thoughts. See yourself as God sees you. Psalm 139:14, gives us the assurance that we are fearfully and wonderfully made. Can't you just imagine God smiling as He made you? Ephesians 2:10, says, "For we are His workmanship, created in Christ Jesus unto good works." This scripture gives us further assurance of our worth.

A few decades ago, there was a catchy phrase that everybody seemed to repeat. It was written on hats, T shirts, mugs, and bumper stickers. It simply said, "I am somebody because God don't make no junk." While it is not scriptural, it is a true saying. Yes, God made all things perfect and beautiful in its time (Ecclesiastes 3:11). If you can just receive that thought in your mind and heart, you can overcome the weight of low self-worth. The value that you put on yourself does not rest with your financial status, level of education, or your past sins. Romans 8:1 lets us know that "there is therefore now no condemnation to them that are in Christ Jesus". Neither is your self-worth determined by who you know or who you don't know!

When you know Christ Jesus as your Lord and savior, then you have an avenue of assurance to have an esteemed life. The words of Lemuel in Proverbs chapter 31 speaks of the virtuous woman. She is priced far above rubies and gold. Her value is priceless. We are priceless to God, as well. Yes, Jesus himself left heaven, and as the Great Shepherd, He will leave the ninety-nine sheep to search you out. He will lift you up and place you in His bosom to bring you into his fold. Whether you are a man or a woman, in God's eyes, you are a treasure. You are a jewel of great price. He gave His life for you. He bought you with His own blood. He told his disciples: "Greater love hath no man than this, that a man lay down his life for his friends" (John 15:13). Yes, Jesus did just that all because of love! God loves you, and that's worth more than anything this world has to offer. Look at yourself and see your worth as God sees it. When God called you out of the womb, His plan was already in place to manifest Himself to you. It doesn't matter what life says about you. You must know, "I am somebody because God don't make junk!"

Prayer:

Heavenly Father, I thank you for being my glory and the "lifter of my head". I confess with my mouth that I am fearfully and wonderfully made, and I am precious in your sight. I cast down all the negative thoughts that the enemy tries to hold over me concerning my past sins. They are like blinders that attempt to hinder me in seeing my true worth. I declare over my life, that I am like that virtuous woman whose price is far above rubies. I thank you, God, that you are helping me to see myself worthy of the price you paid for my sins. You laid down your life for me. Help me to abide in you that you might abide in me because you truly are the one who adds value to my life, In Jesus' name I pray. Amen.

Daily encouragement / Further scripture study and readings:

Monday: Psalm 139:14
Tuesday: Proverbs 3:15
Wednesday: Galatians 4:7
Thursday: Proverbs 10:20
Friday: Jeremiah 29:11
Saturday: Romans 5:8
Sunday: 1 John 4:19

Look Up and Live

"He brought me up also out of a horrible pit, out of the miry clay, and set my feet upon a rock and established my goings." Psalm 40:2

Weight/Sin: **Depression**
(Sadness, Despondency, Hopelessness)

Inspiration:

When Christians find themselves in a "valley experience," it can be perceived as a dreadful place. It is so low, so wide, so barren, and so far from the mountaintop. Valleys seem to be the hardest places for a child of God to go through. Why? Because we are a people of joy and rejoicing! We have the mentality like eagles that are made to fly high and soar. We wish to soar high, dwelling on mountaintops in godly realms and be lifted up in spirit. On the mountaintop, we have a heavenly sight where our views are unobstructed, praying is easy, and answers seem to come speedily.

In the valley the enemy assails and torments our souls. Here the place is dry, and praying seems difficult. The trials we face tend to linger too long. The valley was never meant for people to dwell, but to be strong and to pass through. The psalmist wrote in Psalm 23:4, "Yea, though I walk through the valley…" When you stop in the valley, troubles storm your soul, the journey gets hard, and your joy leaves. Your rejoicing turns into tears and fears. The longer you feel the "valley experience," the more sadness will arise. It does not matter if you are a new believer or a seasoned Christian. Depression can set in to become your ready companion.

LET IT ALL GO! WHAT ARE YOU "WEIGHTING" FOR?

Depression, the condition of sadness, and deep dejection that leaves one low in spirit was experienced by several biblical characters including David, Moses, Job, and Elijah. Proverbs 8:14 affirms the value of coping skills when it speaks of having "sound wisdom." God lets us know, "Counsel is mine and sound wisdom: I am understanding; and have strength." Having coping skills is the wisdom to deal with life's bumps. Being able to cope prevents falling into depression. If you are without this wisdom, ask God for it. The Bible tells us in James 1:5, "If any of you lack wisdom, let him ask of God, that giveth to men liberally and upbraided not; and it shall be given him."

When depression comes, one can certainly find encouragement in the life of Job. Job's suffering became so intense that he described it as being struck by poison arrows from God (Job 6:4). In his saddened state, Job wanted to die. Later in the book of Job, we see a depressed Job confronting God. He spoke honestly to God out of deep anguish. From that conversation came the reassurance of God's love for Job, and Job's love and trust in God. When things happen that threaten to send you into a state of depression, go honestly before God in prayer. God will give you the reassurance of His love and the strength you need to make it through. He will bring you out of your horrible pit. Although, we may not understand why we suffer things in life, we still can know that we serve a great God who has given us mental stability and a sound mind full of power and love. And like Paul, who went through many afflictions such as beatings, shipwrecks, imprisonment, and persecutions, we can still rejoice! Paul advised us to rejoice in all things. The hand of God is on you, and He will deliver you. We are a people that were created to praise God. So, rejoice in the Lord, always! And again, I say rejoice!

Prayer:

Father, I come to you because of the sadness and despondency that I feel. I seek you because you are a wonderful counselor that will help me walk through this difficult time. I thank you for giving me sound wisdom and the strength to move beyond my emotions and trust you. Thank you for your constant love and care. I thank you for lifting this depression from me and helping me to smile again. In Jesus' name I pray. Amen.

Daily encouragement / Further scripture study and readings:

Monday: Psalm 40:1–3
Tuesday: Psalm 42:1–11
Wednesday: Psalm 3:3
Thursday: 1 Peter 5:6–7
Friday Psalm 32:10
Saturday: John 16:33
Sunday: Romans 3:38–39
(also see fear, sadness, depression, dejection)

Putting the Pieces Together Again

"For my life is spent with grief, and my years with sighing: my strength faileth because of mine iniquity, and my bones are consumed. I am forgotten as a dead man out of mind: I am like a broken vessel." Psalm 31:10, 12

Weight/Sin: **Brokenness**
(Helplessness, Hopelessness, Disconnection)

Inspiration:

How did it feel when you broke your most favorite or valued treasure or vase? Perhaps you looked to see if you could fix it. Have you ever broken a cherished heirloom? Did you look for a professional mender, an expert that specializes in mending the broken pieces? You asked if it could be put back in its original state. When a piece is shattered, it is broken beyond repair. The pieces are gathered, the small and large pieces, the bits and slithers are swept up. The once-admired beautiful treasure is thrown away.

Brokenness is the state a person is in when life's pressures have caused a shattering of emotions, pretty much the same way a glass would shatter if hit by a heavy object. Broken people are worn down to a point they can no longer fight. The world seems to discard and reject broken people, but God doesn't: "The Lord is close to the broken-hearted and saves those who are crushed in spirit" (Psalms 34:18, NIV). David, in Psalm 31, describes a time when he was despondent. He was wasting away inside. In describing his feelings to us, David tells of the hopelessness and helplessness that everyone feels when faced with rejection, hatred, and extreme adversity. He sees himself as a broken vessel just like that shattered glass. But, being a man after God's own heart, he knows how to be made whole. He turns to God and calls out to the only one who can save him. David tenderly expresses the love and trust that he has for God.

At the point of brokenness is where you seek God more from the depths of the` heart than from the head. Brokenness may be too much for you to bear, but it is an easy thing for God to mend. Remember that your future is in his hands, and He will help you remain steadfast in your faith. Trust in the God who loves and cares for you regardless of how life's circumstances attempt to leave you broken. We tend to feel, when we are broken, that we are no longer any good. We wonder, can the inside be mended? Can we ever be made whole again? We question our emotions, believing that everything inside of us needs a repair. Only by the grace of God and His infinite mercy can we be healed. Jesus said, "they that are whole need not a physician; but they that are sick" (Luke 5:31). Jesus came to heal the broken hearted. In Christ, we find that every vessel presented to Him, even in a broken state, can be repaired and restored to its original state. He is the expert, the master potter. All God asks is that you come to Him and commit your ways unto Him (Psalm 37:5). Oh, how faithful He is to minister to you! He can heal all of our wounds and mend all our brokenness. It is only Him who can make us vessels of honor meant for the Master's use! (2 Timothy 2:21). To God be the glory!

Prayer:

Father, in the name of Jesus and gracious Lord, I cry unto you out of my brokenness. I give you the shattered and broken pieces of my life. I am trusting you to make me whole again. Thank you for fixing all that is broken within me. I pray, Lord, when I am weak and worn down, come and be my strength. Father, you are helping me to remember that trials and difficulties come to make me strong, not to break me or condemn me. All because of you, I will no longer be disconnected and feel hopeless, but I will look to you to mend my life.

I trust you to be my healer and my savior and my Lord. I will declare to others: "Come and hear, all who fear God, and I will tell what God has done for my soul; I will tell them, when I cried to you with my mouth, high praise was on my tongue. God, you truly have listened and attended to the voice of my prayer. I will declare to all who will listen; Blessed be the God of my salvation, because He has not rejected my prayer or removed His steadfast love from me!" (Psalm 66:16–20, NIV). Lord, I thank You for putting the broken pieces of my life back together again. I thank you for restoration. Amen.

Daily encouragement /Further scripture study and readings:

Monday: Psalm 31:14–18
Tuesday: Psalm 42:6
Wednesday: John 16:33
Thursday: Ephesians 6:12
Friday: Psalm 34:18
Saturday: Psalm 147:3
Sunday: Isaiah 57:15

Less of Me, More of Jesus

"Let nothing be done through strife or vainglory; but in lowliness of mind let each esteem other better than themselves." Philippians 2:3

Weight/Sin: **Overbearing**
(Proud, Dominant, Controlling)

Inspiration:

Of all the female names of the Holy Bible, I have never heard anyone name their precious baby girl Jezebel. That name is associated with the tyrannical, overbearing queen of Israel. King Ahab married this woman of Sidon, and she dominated his throne (1 Kings 16). She controlled the king and his kingdom. She murdered through treachery to get what she wanted, to satisfy her own lusts. She tore down the alters of God and tried to destroy all that was of God. She built temples and erected idols known by her idolatrous nation. She persecuted the prophets of God and killed godly priests. She appointed her own prophets and priest to serve in her temples of idolatry. She was the epitome of an overbearing, dominating, and controlling person.

An overbearing person is one who is masterful, tyrannical, dominant, proud, and loves to rule or control others. An overbearing person has a personality that comes across as harsh, unkind, unloving, and self-centered; a person who usually lacks humility and is less than a team player. Pride should not be the thing that motivates a Christian. Rather, they should be motivated to do everything through the power of the Holy Spirit. A Christian should deal with everyone in humility, which will enable them to value other people above their own personal gains and agendas.

How does one learn to operate in humility? By looking to our Lord and Savior, Jesus Christ. He humbled himself by willingly taking on the role of a servant. No, that does not mean that you are to become a doormat for the wicked to walk on, rather, you become the loving one who will smooth out the rough edges. Start with the way you speak to others. Let your speech always be gracious and seasoned with salt (Colossians 4:6). Look for the value in others and treat them the way that you wish to be treated. John the Baptist understood humility. He was the forerunner for Jesus. He Himself testified speaking of what Jesus said (John 3:19—30). "This is where my joy is fulfilled; He must increase, but I must decrease" (John 3:30). Jesus had come on the scene. The Lord's ministry had begun. John was testifying that he would have to step aside, remove himself from the focal point of attention and let Jesus be the light.

We can release the overbearing nature and take on a modest attitude. We must know that it is time for less of ourselves and more of Jesus. I *must* decrease that He may increase! Seeking and operating in the wisdom of God will eliminate our need to always be in control. Exchange the overbearing spirit for meekness and lowliness of heart because it is the meek that shall inherit the earth. Finally, in the words of my dear late mother, "Be sweet and keep on praying."

Prayer:

Dear Father, teach me to walk in humility in my relationships with others. I humble myself at the foot of the cross that I might receive more of you so that when others look at me, they will see you, not an overbearing and controlling person. I thank you, Lord, that I am learning to relax and rest in you, knowing that I don't need to be in control, because you are in complete control of every aspect of my life. I yield my thoughts, my tongue, and my actions to you. Lord, give me wisdom to speak words that help and not hurt, to heal and not kill, to esteem and not discredit others. Lord, help me to build up others and not tear them down. Use me in such a way that others will see you at work in my life and desire you. I thank you, Lord, that you will renew my mind; and I will be a servant who is profitable in the kingdom of God. In Jesus' name, I pray. Amen.

Daily encouragement /Further scripture study and readings:

Monday: James 3:17–18
Tuesday: Proverbs 21:24
Wednesday: Proverbs 17:27–28
Thursday: Ecclesiastes 8:9
Friday: Titus 3:10
Saturday: 1 Corinthians 1:10
Sunday: Romans 16:17–18

Rejected of Men

"For my father and mother have forsaken me, but the Lord will take me in." Psalm 27:10 (ESV)

Weight/Sin: **Rejection**
(Shunned, Ostracized, Neglected, Denied)

Inspiration:

Jesus was despised and rejected of men. He was a man who suffered many sorrows and was acquainted with grief. He was wounded for our transgressions, bruised for our iniquities, the chastisement of our peace was laid upon him, and with his stripes we are healed (paraphrase of Isaiah 53:3–5). He went to his own, and his own received him not. His brethren and his countrymen did not receive or accept Him. They did not believe that He was the Messiah. The religious leaders of that day, the Sanhedrin counsel, Pharisees and Sadducees were the very men that should have known Him and welcomed him as the Messiah, but they despised Him and rejected Him. In their detestable blindness, they crucified the Lord of glory!

I believe, we all have experienced the pain of rejection. We all have known the ache in our hearts and felt tears sting our eyes at the moment of rejection. Rejection is abrupt dismissal, being rudely ignored, abandoned, verbally attacked, humiliated, and just plain unaccepted. It can deliver emotional punches to the soul and spirit of an individual, leaving brokenness, discouragement, disappointment, and depression. Rejection in any form, on any level, offers nothing but pain. Rejection does not define a person's worth or diminish his value. People are not damaged goods on an assembly "reject" line of life.

John 1:11–12 says, Jesus "came unto his own, and his own received him not. But as many as received him, to them gave he power to become the sons of God, even to them that believe on his name". Jesus died for you. You are valuable to God! You are loved by Him, purchased by the blood of Jesus, and accepted into His family. He has received you and given you power to become a child of the Father. He does not want you to struggle with rejection and your self-worth. Jesus said, "Ye have not chosen Me, but I have chosen you, and ordained you that you should go and bring forth fruit, and that your fruit may remain," (John 15:16). God wants you to be free. Free from the pains of the past; free from disappointments of the present and any grief in the future. If anybody knows rejection, it would be Jesus Christ. He was despised and rejected of men, a man of sorrows, and acquainted with grief.

Prayer

Father, you gave your only begotten Son that whosoever will believe on Him shall not perish but have everlasting life. We know that your son, Jesus, experienced troubles and rejection. He knew sorrows, and grief. He understands what I am facing and what I am going through. He has seen my tears, and He has felt my pain. Sorrow has been my constant companion. Jesus, you said that Satan desired to sift Peter like wheat, and he wishes to do the same with all the saints of God. I know you strengthened Peter and you'll strengthen me.

I repent of all my sins, right now. I repent of all the negative emotions of rejection that I hold in my heart. I understand it has no place in my life. I submit myself under the mighty hand of God. I resist the devil, and he must flee. I am so thankful that you accepted me when others rejected me. I accept the grace of God for my healing. I accept that I am in Christ Jesus. I am a child of God. I believe on Jesus, and I have eternal life. You have accepted me and received me for who I am. Help me to live in love and be accepting of others. Now that I am changed, help me to be a strength in service to my church. I am in you, and you are in me. Together, Lord, we can accomplish mighty things for your kingdom. Bless all I set my hands to do in your Word. And, may the peace that only you can bring, replace the rejection I once knew, in Jesus' name I pray. Amen.

Daily encouragement /Further scripture study and readings:

Monday: John 1:11–12
Tuesday: Psalm 27:10
Wednesday: Psalm 118:22
Thursday: Mark 12:10
Friday: Isaiah 53:3
Saturday: Romans 8:31
Sunday: 1 Samuel 16:1
(Also, see self-worth, depression)

Not Guilty, Case Dismissed

"For I will be merciful to their unrighteousness and their sins and their lawless deeds I will remember no more." Hebrews 8:12 (NKJV)

Weight/Sin: **Guilt**
(Condemnation, Shame, Regret, The Burden of Guilt)

Inspiration:

What is guilt? It is the feeling of remorse when one has committed an offense. The feeling of disgrace when you've violated your own ethical or moral code of conduct; a feeling of heartache, a weight on the spirit from doing wrong. Dealing with guilt seems to be one of the hardest things to do. You may be one who have sinned and failed miserably in many areas of your life; such as: a failed marriage, relationships, friendships, you may have let someone down, caused hurt or pain, been dangerous or destructive to yourself and others or maybe influenced others to fall into sin. Although, you may have tried to hide the guilt of your past, you have not been able to escape the pain.

Roman 3:23 says, "For all have sinned, and come short of the glory of God." We have all messed up! And, we've all made some bad choices in life. The word of God reminds us, "As it is written, there is none righteous, no, not one" (Roman 3:10). That is why we need a savior. In Jesus Christ, we have an advocate with the Father. When we do wrong, we can approach the throne of God. There, we will find that He is a merciful God. Ask for forgiveness and trust Jesus, He is our advocate. He will plead your case to our heavenly Father.

King David was such a man who was found to be full of guilt and condemnation. (His story can be read in 2 Samuel chapter 11). David committed adultery with Uriah's wife, Bathsheba, and she conceived a child from that affair. To cover up for their infidelity, David devised a plan that didn't work out for them. They were sure to be found out. Then David does the unthinkable. Instead of owning up to his treachery and honoring a loyal soldier as Uriah, he ordered Uriah's death. Then, he took Bathsheba to be his wife. Nathan, the prophet, was sent by God to confront David. His sins were found out. He was guilty of coveting, adultery, and murder. He tried to hide it. He tried to make it right, but the sin deed was done. God knew all that was done, yet He still loved David. It was time to accept the responsibility of his actions. David owned up to his offense and poured out his guilt with a repenting heart. Psalm chapter 51 gives insight into the repentant prayer he offered to the Lord. God forgave him, and Nathan was able to counsel him. Although judgment from God for the deeds done by David brought great consequences, he continued to live as a man after God's own heart.

You cannot be effective in Christian ministry holding on to guilt and condemnation. It is a difficult place to be in. How can you move on while living in guilt? Like Nathan confronting David, it must be dealt with. How can you rid yourself of the burden of guilt?

1. Guilt can be dealt with by admitting wrongdoing.
2. Owning your mistakes and accepting the responsibility for your sins.
3. Do not blame anyone for what you've done.
4. Be accountable for your actions.
5. Ask God to forgive your sin, and the person you may have mistreated, as well.

When we ask God to forgive us, we have this promise in 1 John 1:9: "if we confess our sins, He is faithful and just to forgive us of our sins and to cleanse us from all unrighteousness." God has a forgiving nature, and He will not condemn us. Jesus died to set us free from all sin, guilt, and shame. There is no better place to start than in the presence of the One who can wash all sin away and change your life eternally. No matter how you came to your situation or how long you've carried that distressing burden of guilt, God is ready with the solution. His arms are outstretched to you. When God forgives, there is a washing and a regeneration of the soul. You are saved and forgiven. Believe, and by faith, the guilt is washed away. Now you must forgive yourself. Allow yourself to be free from Satan's accusations and from condemnation. "There is, therefore, now no condemnation to them which are in Christ Jesus, who walk not after the flesh, but after the Spirit (Romans 8:1). Your case is dismissed!

Prayer:

Father, I confess my guilt to you. You are a holy and merciful God. I humble myself before you with my grief-stricken spirit and a remorseful heart. I repent, and I call on the name of the Lord to be made whole. Forgive me of my wrongdoing. Cleanse me from secret faults, secret sins, and all unrighteousness. A broken and contrite spirit you will not despise. A lowly and humble person you will not turn away. Help me and keep me from doing wrong. I am broken before you, Lord. I relinquish the guilt of my past sins. I relinquish the shame of my countenance. Free me of this burden of guilt and condemnation. I have decided, I will not go back into the bondage of guiltiness.

Thank you, Lord, for the truth that I am saved by your grace and I am no longer a slave to sin. The truth has set me free. I have this promise, whom the Son makes free, is free indeed. I welcome the works of the Holy Spirit into my life to cleanse me and fill me with power from on high. Help me to not walk after my flesh but walk after your Holy Spirit. Lead me into all truth, for your Word is true. Order my steps according to your Word. I pray that the river of living waters will flow over my life once again. Holy Spirit, flow to every area of my life bringing healing and liberty. Restore unto me the joy I once knew. The joy that is unspeakable and full of glory that I may rejoice in the joy of my salvation once again. Lord, you are my burden bearer, and my redeemer, and you paid my sin debt.

Sin has no dominion over me. The chains of guilt and condemnation are broken from me, and I have been set free. There is now no condemnation to those who are in Christ Jesus. I will not live under shame. I will live in freedom. I will live for you, Lord. In Jesus' name I pray. Amen.

Daily encouragement /Further scripture study and readings:

Monday: Romans 8:1
Tuesday: 1 John 1:9
Wednesday: 1 Corinthians 10:13
Thursday: Acts 8:22
Friday: Acts 3:19
Saturday John 3:17
Sunday: Hebrews 10:14–17

Who Told You That You Were Naked?

"For the Lord God will help me; therefore, shall I not be confounded; Therefore, have I set my face like a flint, and I know that I shall not be ashamed." Isaiah 50:7

Weight/Sin: **Shame**
(Embarrassment, Humiliation, Disgraced)

Inspiration:

Adam and Eve knew God. They knew His voice and His presence. After they had eaten from the tree of knowledge of good and evil, their eyes were open to evil, sin, and shame. They experienced the good of life. They lived in the garden of Eden; a land God created for them. They had fellowship with God, and they lived in peace. They were whole, covered in the glory, and they walked in the light of God. Genesis 2:25 reads, "And they were both naked, the man and his wife, and were not ashamed." Unfortunately, for the whole human race, the great deceiver clothed himself as a serpent and deceived Adam and Eve, and they disobeyed the directions of God. They ate of the tree from which they were instructed not to eat, and sin entered God's creation. In their disobedience, their eyes were indeed opened; their transgressions were exposed, the human race was infected with a sinful nature, and they had the knowledge of evil.

For the first time, they saw themselves without the glory of the God. The light was gone. They looked at themselves, and they saw that they were exposed and uncovered. They were naked, and they were ashamed. They covered themselves with fig leaves. They hid themselves. God came to fellowship with them. God called out to Adam, "Where art thou?" In his shame, he answered by explaining, "I heard you coming. We were naked, so we hid." God asked, "Who told you, that you were naked? Have you eaten from the tree I warned you about?" Genesis 3:9–11 They did eat of the fruit. They stood before their creator no longer under glory, but shame. They saw and experienced the good of all God created. Now, their eyes were open to immorality and sin.

Have you ever been so ashamed of what you've said or done that all you want to do is crawl away somewhere and hide? Or just drop dead from embarrassment right there on the spot? Have you been so humiliated that you didn't want to face spectators, your peers, or anyone? Oh, how you wished at that moment that you could stop the time and have a do-over. Then you can erase that very moment of humiliation.

In life, there is no do-over! There is no stop, pause, or rewind buttons in life. Once your words have been spoken or the deed is done, there is just no taking it back. God's love is long-suffering. Love covers a multitude of sins, even shame. Who told you that you were naked? Who is behind all deception? Who is the influence that will hold you in shame? It is the devil! The deceiver! The accuser! It is Satan, and he does not want you healed! He doesn't want you delivered from your past failures.

When you were saved, you were delivered from past sins. If you hold on to shame, then you hold on to unbelief that God saved you, cleansed you, and washed all your sins away. One of the benefits as a born-again believer is to know that Christ has blotted out all your transgressions. Jesus wants you delivered and free. Isaiah 50:7 reads, "For the Lord God will help me; therefore, shall I not be confounded: therefore, have I set my face like a flint, and I know that I shall not be ashamed." Christ died to set you free of whatever shame you may be facing that you won't let go. Look to Jesus, and by faith, trust Him to bring you deliverance and victory over shame. Release your pride. Don't allow pride to hold you captive. Humble yourself, be wise, and be free. Proverbs 11:2, "When pride cometh, then cometh shame: but with the lowly is wisdom."

In Jesus Christ, you have been set free. Believe in this truth; you are covered by the blood of Jesus. Satan has nothing on you! You can stand naked and unashamed in the presence of God. Put on spiritual garments, clothe yourself in His righteousness, and be crowned with His glory! You have nothing to hide. There is nothing between you and God, and no reason to hide from His presence. Your sins are forgiven and blotted out. God will not hold them against you anymore. They are removed as far from you as the east is to the west. They are forgiven and forgotten. Hebrews 12:2 says, "Looking unto Jesus the author and finisher of our faith; who for the joy that was set before Him endured the cross, despising the shame, and is set down at the right hand of the throne of God." Jesus endured the cross, the shame, and the humiliation because of the joy that was to come. The joy of returning to His throne in glory to be an advocate for mankind. The joy of seeing the redemption plan in operation. The joy that He will have in the fellowship once again with man. You can't go into your future while holding on to the past. Release that shame and be forgiven. Joy awaits you!

Prayer:

Father, just as Peter wept bitterly, I too have shed many tears over the disgrace I feel. I humble myself before you, Lord. You said in your Word, if I humble myself before you, Lord, you shall exalt me in due season. I release this shame and ask to be forgiven. Deliver me, Lord, and heal my brokenness. Only you can mend the past and weave my future. I put down the lies of the enemy, and I am renewing my mind. Jesus, you are the author and finisher of my faith. I look to you, and I know that you are working all things together for my good. I empty myself out before you and stand naked and unashamed in your presence. I shall come out of this place of embarrassment and shame. I lay aside all pride and self-seeking validations and pick up humility.

I am justified only through Christ Jesus who is the justifier. I have been through the trial of this weight like it was fire. I thank you for the promise, they that are tried by fire shall come forth as pure gold. Make me pure and holy, Lord. The beauty of your holiness shall rise from the ashes of my despair. By faith, I shall move into my joy and into your glory. There is joy for me on the other side of this valley of shame. I thank you that I am free from shame today. Hallelujah, in Jesus' name. Amen.

Daily encouragement /Further scripture study and readings:

Monday: Proverbs 11:2
Tuesday: Hebrews 12:2
Wednesday: Isaiah 54:4
Thursday: 1 Corinthians 6:5
Friday: Philippians 3:18–20
Saturday: Acts 5:4
Sunday: Genesis 3:9–10
(Also, see pride, guilt)

A Sorrowful Spirit

"The Lord is near to the brokenhearted and saves the crushed in spirit." Psalm 34:18 (ESV)

Weight/Sin: **Grievous**
(Heartache, Agony, Sorrowful, Mournfulness)

Inspiration:

1Samuel chapters 1 and 2 tell the story of Hannah and her plight. Hannah's husband was Elkanah. He had two wives, Hannah and Penninah. Although, Elkanah was the head of his household, the relationship between his wives was strained. The Word expressed that he loved Hannah, but she was barren. Was Hannah his first wife? Was it because she was barren that he took a second wife? It was Penninah who bore him children. Elkanah and his family annually traveled from their home in Ramah to the tabernacle in Shiloh to worship. There, they'd offer their required sacrifices for atonement and attend the festivals. Every year, they went up to the temple, and every year, Hannah was persistently grief-stricken by Penninah. Not only was she constantly reminded by the children of her husband that she was barren, she was also ridiculed by their mother. She tormented Hannah, taunted her, laughed at her, and scorned her to shame. Hannah would cry, becoming physically sick, and unable to eat. Grievousness became her meat and tears her drink. Even the loving words of her husband could not comfort the deep sorrow of her soul. She had a sorrowful spirit. Hannah lived in this grievous condition for years. She wrestled with this torment year after year.

LET IT ALL GO! WHAT ARE YOU "WEIGHTING" FOR?

During the annual festivities, after their sacrifices were offered at the temple, Hannah went to the altar. She dealt with her broken heart the only way she knew how: she took it to the Lord! She was found in the temple by the priest Eli on her knees agonizing in prayer. She was in deep anguish, crying bitterly, and pouring out all her sorrow. She was moving her lips, but no words came out. Eli thought she was drunk with wine. She said to him, "No, my lord, I am a woman of a sorrowful spirit; I have not drunk neither wine nor strong drink, but I have poured out my soul before the Lord." She emptied her grief and pain onto the altar. She was at a point where she wasn't concerned with what onlookers may have seen or thought of her. She prayed. She poured out her petitions before God. And, God heard her cry. The priest Eli answered and said, "Go in peace and the God of Israel grant thee thy petition that thou has asked of Him" (1 Samuel 1:17). She left the temple healed. Life doesn't seem fair when you've experienced great sorrow and suffering at the hand of another. A grievous burden is something you do not have to carry. 1Peter 5:7 lets us know, we can cast all our cares upon Jesus, because He cares for us. God may seem far away at times, but the truth is He is with you. He promised to give to us one that will abide with us forever. "Jesus prayed to the Father and said He shall give you another comforter. A comforter that will abide with you and live inside of you," (John 14:16–17). Jesus is as close as His name.

Hannah, like so many others, endured harsh treatment and hurtful words (even if the words were true). Grievousness overwhelmed her life. It consumed her soul. Just as David cried out to God, so should we: "From the end of the earth will I cry unto thee, Oh Lord, when my heart is overwhelmed, lead me to the rock that is higher than I." As you read the outcome in Hannah's story, you will see that misery does not have to dictate the outcome of your future. There is help for your healing in Jesus. Saints, God has already given you a future full of hope and success (Jeremiah 29:11). He is ready to hear your prayer, answer your cry, and heal your deep-seated sorrow. Like Hannah, you may have suffered a great deal, maybe for a long time, but there is a place to find help in your hour of great need. Take it to the Lord in prayer.

Prayer:

Father, I bare my soul to you. Grievousness has overwhelmed and consumed my life. Sadness and sorrow have followed me for many days. You are my rock in a weary land, a shelter from the storms, and my strong and mighty high tower. You are the Father of mercies and the God of all comfort. You comfort all who mourn in Zion. Dear Lord, heal my pain, heal my grieving. In you, I put all my trust. I trust your Word that says your people may go out weeping, dragging their sheaves behind them, but shall without doubt come again, returning to their place in you with rejoicing. It may seem far off right now, but you are the lifter of my head and the light of my countenance. Weeping may endure for a night, but my joy shall come in the morning. I take off the garment of heaviness, and I put on the garment of praise. And as I move from this place of sorrow, I will rise from the ashes into the beauty of your holiness. You have a plan for me, a hope, and a future. I release the sorrow right now and ask that you heal my broken spirit. I pray these things, Father, in Jesus's name. Amen.

Daily encouragement /Further scripture study and readings:

Monday: Psalm 61:2
Tuesday: Psalm 69:29
Wednesday: 1 Samuel 1:15
Thursday: Matthew 19:20–22
Friday: Matthew 26:38
Saturday: 2 Corinthians 6:1–10
Sunday: John 14:16
(also, see grief, hatred, jealousy)

Let God Exalt You!

"Pride goes before destruction, a haughty Spirit before a fall." Proverbs 16:18 (ESV)

Weight/Sin: **High-Minded**
(Proud, Haughty, Conceited, Overconfident)

Inspiration:

High-minded and haughty are not common words in today's vernacular. However, they are used in several scriptures in the Holy Bible. The words high-minded and haughty come as a rebuke and a warning to the proud, arrogant, and puffed-up person. "Pride goeth before destruction", it says in Proverbs and a "haughty spirit before a fall. Better it is to be of a humble spirit with the lowly than to divide the spoil with the proud" (Proverbs 16:18–19). "These six things doth the Lord hate: yea, seven are an abomination unto him: a proud look, a lying tongue, and hands that shed innocent blood, a heart that deviseth wicked imaginations, feet that be swift in running to mischief, a false witness that speaketh lies, and he that soweth discord among brethren" (Proverbs 6:16–19). "Haughty eyes, a proud heart and evil actions are all sin" Proverbs 21:4 (NLT). Although, a person can show humility on the outside, the heart can be decisively wicked.

In such a case, we read about the religious leaders of the Sanhedrin, Pharisees, and Sadducees in the gospels. They had the outward appearance of humble, stout, and righteous men. They taught humility, but their hearts were proud and wicked. They lifted themselves above the very ones who needed their help, sinners, the sick, and the outsiders. Their responsibilities to the people demanded a mission of servitude, but their attitudes were far from serving others. Paul wrote this explanation to the Roman church: "For I say through the grace given unto me, to every man that is among you, not to think of himself more highly than he ought to think; but to think soberly, according as God hath dealt to every man the measure of faith" (Romans 12:3). He is saying, rather, judge yourself with clearheaded judgment according to the measure of faith God has given you.

Do not be puffed up, prideful, arrogant, and haughty. Do not think more highly of yourself than you ought. Do not be boastful and lifted up in yourself because it is by the grace of God that we are who we are. The root of being high-minded, of course, is pride and exalting self. It is not of God to boast of your talents, positions, riches, and abilities. Wasn't it God who gave the talent as a gift? Wasn't it God who granted the promotion? Wasn't it God who blessed man to get wealth? Where does pride really come from? Exaltation in a proud, high-minded, arrogant way is a lie from Satan. Paul said for us to judge ourselves truthfully, because God gave us everything we have, and it is for our enjoyment. He gave us all our wealth, talents, positions, and ministries. Without Christ, we are nothing; but with Him, we are the sons of God. We can honor him by giving back to Him all the praise and glory that is due Him.

I am reminded of the one that was so proud and lifted up that he desired to take all the glory and praise from God for himself. Dare I mention his name? Lucifer! Isaiah 14:12–15 describes so vividly the rise and fall of Satan. "How art thou fallen from heaven O' Lucifer, son of the morning! How art thou cut down to the ground, which didst weaken the nations! For thou hast said in thine heart, I will ascend into heaven, I will exalt my throne above the stars of God: I will sit also upon the mount of the congregation, in the sides of the north: I will ascend above the heights of the clouds; I will be like the Most High." Pride is Satan's sin. Jesus testifies that he witnessed the demise of Lucifer. He said in Luke 10:18, "I beheld Satan as lightning fall from heaven."

A haughty spirit that willfully opposes God is in great error, and this will surely bring judgment. Take heed, God's Word is truth!

LET IT ALL GO! WHAT ARE YOU "WEIGHTING" FOR?

Remember, "Pride goes before destruction, and a haughty spirit before a fall. Better to be of a humble spirit with the lowly than to divide the spoil with the proud" (Proverbs 16:18–19). Let us never be too proud that we don't see our need to depend on God. "Humble yourselves therefore under the mighty hand of God, that he may exalt you in due time" (1 Peter 5:6).

Prayer:

Heavenly Father, soberly and honestly, I judge myself according to your Word. Haughty eyes, a proud heart, and evil actions are all sin. It is time for me to repent of a high-minded attitude and this haughty spirit. How dare me to look upon others with condescending ways? This pride found in me is no longer desired of me. Jesus died as the ransom for all. And, it is only by the grace of God that I am who I am.

Wash me, Lord. Cleanse me by the blood of Jesus and renew the right spirit within me. I renew my mind in the Holy Ghost. I crucify my flesh, and I'll abstain from evil. God of peace sanctify me wholly, my whole spirit, soul, and body. Preserve me that I may be blameless at the coming of the Lord, Jesus Christ. I fear the Lord. Keep my feet from stumbling. Keep me in all my ways as I commit them to you. Satisfy my mouth with good things and grant me long life. I honor you, oh God, for who you are. You are the God of all creation, and, the hope of all the earth. As Your love surrounds me, let me minister your love to others. Help me to be a blessing to those in need. Let me lead the way and make paths clear that souls might be saved. I will lift up the name of Jesus and I will exalt your name forever. Forgive me and restore me to do your will. In Jesus' name I pray. Amen.

Daily encouragement /Further scripture study and readings:

Monday: Proverbs 6:16–19
Tuesday: Proverbs 8:13
Wednesday: Proverbs 21:4
Thursday: Romans 12:3

Friday: 1 Timothy 6:17
Saturday: Isaiah 2:11
Sunday: Isaiah 14:12–15
(also, see pride)

Careful, Giants Do Fall!

"For God hath not given us the spirit of fear; but of power, and of love and of a sound mind."
2 Timothy 1:7

Weight/Sin: **Intimidation**
(Terrorized, Browbeaten, Threatened, Scared)

Inspiration:

    Track-and-field is just one of the many spring sports that demonstrates the speed, agility, and the endurance of an athlete. I overheard a conversation of a group of young men that were preparing to warm up before a race. I sat and watched as they greeted the newcomers and renewed acquaintances from previous meets. They discussed their status, their running times, and how they placed at former meets. They talked about a young athlete who was fast and good. They all admired him. They spoke of how they knew they could never beat him in the hurdles event. Year after year, he became faster. He had the best running time at the state meet the year before. Their coaches used his time as a bench mark when they practiced. They all told how they came up short in their personal time against his time. I was surprised that they spoke this way. They were intimidated by this good athlete. But, more surprisingly, I saw they were defeated before they ever started the race!
    Intimidation creates feelings of fear, awe, or inadequacy to persuade or discourage by causing fear, *(to persuade somebody to do something or dissuade somebody from doing something by frightening them)*. We create the feelings of inadequacy in ourselves when we compare

ourselves to others, like the young athletes in the story. They dwelt and focused on how they measured up to one another. In comparison, they did not *see* themselves as champions. If their coaches could have heard the conversation, I believe the first thing he would do when they were back in training, would be to change their way of thinking. He would first start to train the athletes to think of themselves as winners by changing their mind-sets.

I love the story of David and Goliath in 1 Samuel chapter 17. King Saul and the whole army of Israel were stifled by the threats of the Philistine army for 110 days. They were propositioned and intimidated by their champion warrior; a giant named Goliath. A teenager named David was sent by his father to the army camp to deliver rations to his brothers. He heard the blasphemy and the threats of Goliath. He accepted the challenge. He went out to meet this enemy with no body armor, no sword, and no shield. He had a sling shot and five rocks. Goliath mocked, taunted, scorned, defied the army of Israel, and blasphemed their God. David boldly declared to Goliath, "You come to me with a sword, and a spear, and with a shield: but I come to you in the name of the Lord of hosts and the God of the armies of Israel whom thou have defied. I will feed your carcass to the fowls of the air and to the beast of the field." David used a rock and his sling shot and knocked Goliath flat to the ground. Then he used the giant's own sword to take off his head. The Philistine army ran in terror, and Israel defeated their enemy!

David was not the likely contender in man's eyes, but he was in the eyes of God. He had to look *really small* to all that were watching, especially, when he stood up against a giant. God used a boy full of faith and courage to slay a giant and defeat a mighty army!

God used what seemed to be the weak to confuse the wise (1Corinthian 1:17). Deuteronomy 31:6: says, "Be strong and of good courage, fear not, nor be afraid of them, for the Lord, thy God it is He that doth go with thee; He will not fail thee, nor forsake thee." Numerous enemies, mighty armies, giants, men of reputation, fenced and fortified cities are nothing to God. There is no place for intimidation in God's people. With God, all things are possible. Our big things are small things to Him. David saw a big man, but he knew God to be bigger. To

LET IT ALL GO! WHAT ARE YOU "WEIGHTING" FOR?

God, our enemies, our troubles, and our problems are nothing. It is up to us not to give place to the devil! Give no place to intimidation! Shut the door on fear and defeat; open the door to faith and success because God has not given us a spirit of fear. When we trust God, he will fulfill every promise, and He will bring victory in every battle!

Prayer:

Father, in Jesus' name, give me the courage to be an overcomer. You are my strength and my salvation. You are the God of my life, so whom shall I fear? I recognize that it is the trick of the enemy to bring insecurities into my view. I give no place to the devil or to intimidation. I resist it, and it must flee. I ask for forgiveness for holding on to fear. I will not be afraid. You have not given me a spirit of fear, but of power, and of love, and of a sound mind. With the help of the Holy Spirit, I submit myself unto you. I cast down every thought and imagination that try to exalt itself before the knowledge of God. I am strong in the Lord and operate in the power of His might. I suit up in the whole armor of God that I may withstand all the fiery darts of the enemy. I stand with my shield of faith and with my sword, which is the Word of God. I am victorious in every battle. I am victorious in you, Lord! I stand equipped with your strength, and in your might. I desire to fulfill the plans and purposes you have set for my life that I may reach my destiny in Christ. I thank you, Lord, that you have never failed me nor forsaken me. Amen.

Daily encouragement /Further scripture study and readings:

Monday: 1 John 4:17–18
Tuesday: 2 Corinthian 1:17
Wednesday: Deuteronomy 31:6
Thursday: 2 Corinthians 11:20
Friday: 1 Peter 5:8
Saturday: Ephesians 6:9
Sunday: Philippians 1:6
(also, see fear, doubt)

I Am Not Afraid

"So, do not fear, for I am with you; do not be dismayed, for I am your God. I will strengthen you and help you; I will uphold you with my righteous right hand." Isaiah 41:10 (NIV)

Weight/Sin: **Timid**
(Fearful, Faint-Hearted, Nervous, Shy)

Inspiration:

Timid is defined as unassertive, not confident, demonstrating a lack of courage, and the lack of self-assurance. Only in cartoons and comedy performances do we laugh at a timid lion, because that is not his nature. The lion, even in captivity, is a wild and fierce animal. The lion of the Saharan lands in Africa, is one of the largest cats in the animal kingdom. The size of an adult male lion is a massive six to eight feet in length (not including the tail). He is an average of four feet in height from ground to shoulder. With its head lifted, it adds about another foot. He weighs from 420 to 600 pounds. According to Wikipedia, a lion's roar is 108 to 114 decibels and can be heard up to five miles away. (The human ears can be damaged at 84 decibels.).

Paul charged the young man, Timothy, to be the overseer for the church at Ephesus. He wrote to warn him of the bombardment from gainsayers, false teachers, and persecutors. He encouraged Timothy to "let no man despise your youth, but be an example for the believers in Word, in conversation, in love, in sprit, in faith and in purity" (1Timothy 4:12). Timothy was quite young for a pastor, and it was insinuated that he was timid, maybe even bashful. Although, he was taught and trained under the guidance of the Apostle Paul, he was an inexperienced leader. The elders of the congregation challenged his authority, his ability, and possibly, questioned his maturity. Paul reminded him, to stay strong in the Lord and operate in the power of His might. Stay true to the ministry and to the call. Follow God and not man. Teach the Word in love and obey the leading of the Spirit. It is not in your ability that you minister, but by the anointing from the Spirit of God. Finally, Paul encouraged him to stir up the gifts that were within him. "For God did not give you a spirit of fear (timidity), but of power and of love and a sound mind" (2 Timothy 1:7). Timothy was ordained to lead the church at Ephesus in all power and authority of God.

Timidity is the opposite of what God desires for His children. Gideon was called a mighty man of valor before he exhibited any signs of bravery. In fact, he was hiding in a winepress when the angel of the Lord appeared to him. These men, Timothy and Gideon, are examples for us to learn that with man, things seem impossible, but through God, all things are possible. Warfare is not for the timid. We are called to be bold in the Lord and in the power of His might. To trust in His might and not in our own. In Christ, we are men and women of valor. We are called to be bold in the Lord, to step out by faith, but it is fear that will stop the move of God. Coyness comes to discourage. Over thinking and under thinking will *think* you right out of God's plan! Sometimes, we can be so careful and cautious that we don't want to trust in our next move or next step. And, eventually, we will doubt God's direction.

What is it that God called you to do? How will you respond? How has the enemy deceived you? How has Satan, the devil gotten the advantage over you? Like Timothy and Gideon, mighty man of valor, turn your timidity into boldness. Get a true focus on the gifts within you and stir them up! Set your face like flint, and don't waver, don't doubt your ability or be moved from where God placed you. Look to what the Word says, "Behold, I give you power to tread over all power of the enemy, and nothing shall by any means harm you" (Luke 10:19). It is for us to understand the power that the Holy Spirit has afforded us over darkness, and to understand our position in ministry. Declare today that you are done with timidity with a steadfast declaration, "I shall not be cowardly, but I will be true to my call."

We are in spiritual warfare. We have battles to fight and victories that need to be won. God has given us all things that we need to be victorious in this life. He has well-equipped us with our weapons of warfare. "For the weapons of our warfare are not carnal, but mighty through God to the pulling down of strongholds (2 Corinthians 10:4). It is time for the Christians to suit up and take this land for the Kingdom of God. We have weapons, armor, and God is on our side. We are victorious in Christ Jesus! If God is for you, who can be against you? Through Jesus Christ, we are triumphant!

Prayer:

Dear heavenly Father, in the name of Jesus, I thank you that I have been equipped with everything I need for ministry and for warfare. Forgive me for being so timid. Forgive me for being fearful. Forgive my apprehension in the church and in service. Forgive my procrastinating. Let me not be so cautious that I miss a God-given opportunity to win the lost. Help me to recognize my weapons and use what Jesus has provided for me and all saints. Help me to resist the enemy of my soul. I rebuke the deceiver. I know that he is as a roaring lion trying to devour my faith and steal my courage. Satan is a liar and the father of them all. He comes for nothing but to steal, kill, and destroy. But, Lord, you came to give me life and that more abundantly.

I am forgetting those things which are behind me, and I shall reach for the things before me. I press toward the mark that I may obtain the prize of the high calling of God in Christ Jesus. I declare today that I am bold in the Lord and in the power of His might. I am courageous! Through God, I shall do valiantly.

In the name of Jesus, I shall rise and go forward. Lord, open my eyes that I may see the opposition before me. Increase my faith. For greater is He that is within me than he that is in the world. Help me to be strong, not in my own strength, but in the strength of the

Lord. I encourage myself in the Lord. I give you honor, oh Lord, and all the praise. I stir up the Holy Spirit that's within me. I stir up the gifts that you bestowed upon me. Through the blood of Jesus Christ, I am set free, and I am victorious. For I have been made more than a conqueror through Him who loves me. Amen.

Daily encouragement /Further scripture study and readings:

Monday: 2 Timothy 1:7
Tuesday: 1 John 4:18
Wednesday: Ephesians 6:10–11
Thursday: Romans 8:1
Friday: Revelation 12:11
Saturday: Exodus 3:11–14
Sunday: Judges 6:14–15
(See fear, intimidation, doubt, anxiety)

From Sadness to Service

"My soul is weary with sorrow; strengthen me according to your word." Psalm 119:28 (NIV)

Weight/Sin: **Sadness**
(Sorrow, Misery, Grief, Depression, Unhappy)

Inspiration:

God created us with the ability to feel emotions. Sadness is just one emotion that has been experienced by everyone at one time or another. It is perfectly natural to feel sadness after experiencing an event that caused loss or injury, but it should not overwhelm you. It is a tactic of Satan to bring misery after one has been low in spirit. He will torment you with sadness and grief. He wants you to believe you will never feel anything but despair. Satan is a liar! He desires to have you as his own and to "sift you as wheat" (Luke 22:31). Ultimately, this will stop you from serving God. You can overcome the weight of sadness through the power of God's Word.

Nehemiah was a cupbearer to King Artaxerxes of Medo-Persia. Never had he served the king in sadness. A sad countenance or expression is an outward appearance of inward sorrow. Sadness of heart is a pit you find yourself in and don't see a way out. Notice, in Nehemiah the first chapter, there were men of Judah that informed and updated Nehemiah on the progress and condition of his people and the work that was being done to rebuild his homeland, Jerusalem. The work wasn't going so well.

The people that returned to restore the city and its fortified walls were trying to work but were met with great opposition. They suffered repeated attacks from their enemies. The news grieved him. He wept, mourned before God. "Sorrow is better than laughter. For by the sadness of the countenance the heart is made better" (Ecclesiastes 7:3). Nehemiah was sad. This wasn't a time for laughter nor a time to dance. He could not be there to help the workers in any way. The sadness of his heart caused him to fast and pray and intercede for his fellow kinsmen. It motivated him to seek the Lord for the safety of the workers and for answers. What else could he do while being in captivity and the king's chief cupbearer?

Nehemiah's past service to the king was in excellence. So the king noticed when his service wasn't in the usual manner. He entered his presence to serve him wine with a sad expression. "Wherefore, the king said unto me, Why is thy countenance sad, seeing thou *art* not sick? This *is* nothing else but sorrow of heart. Then, I was sore afraid" (Nehemiah 2:2). It wasn't to get attention or to make others pity him, but his spirit was grieved, and his heart was sad. He was a slave, and therefore, he was afraid. He could be abolished if he offended the king in any way. He was favored by the king. So, the king granted him his request to go help his fellow countrymen (Nehemiah 2:1–6).

When a spirit of sadness lingers, we must remember how good God is to us. There is a sadness that is lingering on the spirit of God's people, a sorrow of heart like a people with no hope. It is there when you wake and when you lie down to sleep. The enemy brought you low and has harassed you with sadness and gloom. He conveys a spirit of hopelessness. He wants you to believe you will never feel anything but despair. You have prayed, cried, and prayed some more. You fasted and humbled yourself before God. You prayed every prayer you know how to pray. You've read the Bible and tried to apply the "ten steps" to perfect faith living. You've tried prayer lines, sent in prayer requests, you've tried sowing a seed, sought counsel from friends, doctors, and the pastor. The sadness is still there, and it just seems like God has not heard you, and your prayers are not reaching heaven.

When things have not changed for you and nothing has moved in your favor, let me reassure you, God has already heard your cry! He is a God of love and mercy. We are not a hopeless people. We have a hope and a victory in Christ Jesus. He is our victory and our exceedingly great reward. The king noticed Nehemiah and gave him favor. Let me tell you, King Jesus has noticed you! He is your intercessor who is seated at the right hand of our Father, and He is interceding on your behalf. God has noticed you! Let the spirit of God be birthed out of this sadness. He has a purpose for you that's full of joy and a strength that'll influence your life. Pray for success and the love of God to prevail over all the enemy's plans. Psalm 16:11, "Thou will show me the path of life: For in the presence of God there is fullness of joy; and at thy right hand there are pleasures evermore." A joyful heart is communicated through our countenance, so we should display gladness for what God has done for us, and it will be reflected in a cheerful disposition. This helps with our witness to Christ and the salvation He brings. Lift your head, child of God! Let the redeemed of the Lord say so! We are redeemed!

In the face of the enemy, give a shout of praise. Give a Hallelujah shout that our God reigns. Don't look at your circumstances because to God, it doesn't matter what it looks like. Don't give ear to Satan because it doesn't matter what the devil has thrown at you and placed in your path. Isaiah 54:17 says, "No weapon formed against you shall prosper, and every tongue that rises against you in judgement, you shall condemn. This is the heritage of the saints, says the Lord". God will be glorified in your situation. He will be exalted above your enemies because God cannot fail. He is your strength and your song, and He is your salvation. When you see no way out, remember, Jesus is the way, the truth, and He is life. He has already made a way of escape. He will not leave you to be prey to the enemy. He will rescue you, bring you out, and God will be glorified. This brokenness you feel today, only God can fix it, and He shall! Wait upon the Lord and be of good courage. Again, I say, wait upon the Lord.

Prayer:

Father, in the name of Jesus, when sadness has overtaken my countenance and I cannot seem to overcome this trial, I pray for strength and power. I have strayed from the real focus and the call of the Holy Spirit. I refuse to be ashamed of the gospel of Jesus Christ because it is the power of God unto salvation to all that'll believe. I hear you calling me back into a place in you. I will return to my first love. I am seeking you, Lord, and returning to the God of my childhood. There I will find peace and joy. You are merciful, mighty and faithful to deliver me from all my distresses. I am coming back to that secret place that I once knew in you.

God, you have called me to be a warrior in the kingdom. I rebuke this sadness. It is a torment and a lie from the pit of hell. I ask that out of this sadness be birthed what you ordained for me, before I was born and before the foundations of the world were spoken into place. I ask for the joy of the Lord to be restored into my life. I am anointed of you to continue to run this race set before me. I am anointed to pray and intercede for my family, loved ones, and as many as you lay on my heart. I answer the call, and I choose to be bold in you. I have the Spirit of God in my heart. I am covered in your glory. I will lift my countenance to you, oh Lord, and decree no more sadness, no more worries. I submit every situation in my life into your hands. The gifts and the call on my life are without repentance. You didn't take them back, and the good work you have started in me, you are faithful to complete it. I lift my head today and face the tasks you have set before me. I have power in the name of Jesus, and I can do all things through Christ who gives me the strength! Amen.

Daily encouragement /Further scripture study and readings:

Monday: Ecclesiastes 7:3
Tuesday: Isaiah 54:17
Wednesday: Hebrews 11:6
Thursday: John 14:1
Friday: Psalm 16:11
Saturday: John 5:14–15
Sunday: Psalm 34:18
(also, see worry, anxiety, grief)

Speak Easy, Speak Clearly

"Pray that I will proclaim this message as clearly as I should." Colossians 4:4 (NIV)

Weight/Sin: **Poor Communicator**
(Incomprehensible, Unclear, Inarticulate)

Inspiration:

God has given mankind the awesome ability to use language to communicate. Our words help us to express our thoughts, feelings, and disposition. God is a communicator. He speaks clearly. Through His words, we can know Him, understand who He is, how to live a good and Godly life, and have eternal life through Christ Jesus. The book of Genesis to Revelations communicates God's plan and His will for man. John 1:1 reads, "In the beginning was the Word, and the Word was with God and the Word was God." The spoken word, the written word, and the spiritual word is still with us. God communicates through His spirit and the written word, and we talk to Him through prayer. With the written word, He leaves no questions unanswered on how to have eternal life.

How important are your words? How important is it to get your point across? How important is it to express yourself wisely? In preaching, building a bridge, a friendship, cooking, baking a cake, designing, instructions, and construction, even in teaching a child to tie their shoes; anything for that matter, that will require you to relate to others, being a good communicator is a necessity.

Once when taking a speech class, I remember one point the professor repeatedly stressed was, "In effective communications, we have to speak to be understood and listen to understand." It was not a direct quote from the Bible, but Proverbs 4:7, tells us, "Wisdom is the principal thing. Therefore, get wisdom: and with all your getting get an understanding." A poor communicator cannot convey his point across to the listener, or the listener may not always hear, understand, or comprehend what is spoken. God gave us His Word for us to flourish and to prosper in it. We cannot flourish or prosper if we do not understand what is being said or what is required from us. Yet, in all our shortcomings God is still good, patient, and long-suffering with us.

The words we speak can cause hurt to others either intentionally or inadvertently. We must be careful to use our words to encourage one another and not tear each other down. When we speak, our speech should be with clarity, directed with grace. "Let your speech always be gracious, seasoned with salt, so that you may know how you ought to answer each person" (Colossians 4:6, ESV).

A poor communicator cannot get a job done successfully. A man or woman who does not know how to tame his tongue, the Word says, is like a ship that is tossed on the waters that cannot be controlled. The tongue is an unruly evil. Out of the mouth proceeds blessing and cursing. Christians should always be aware of what we say *and* how we say it when communing with others. We are people of the faith. A people that should not be wavering, speaking to our shame and being double-minded. James 1:8 says, "He that is double-minded is unstable in all his ways." And the man who wavers and doubts, let him know that he'll receive nothing from God. A wise man spoke these words: "An angry man who curses and swears has exhausted his vocabulary." Speaking foolishly and being a vain babbler has no edification. When the flesh rules the tongue, then no one benefits. Let us never speak out of anger, disrespect, or stupidity. It is for us to be wise and diligent. There is much to do in the kingdom of God. As we work together in unity, may we be led by the spirit of God and not by the flesh.

Remember, as Christians we are to always follow the example of Christ in all that we do, including how we communicate with others. I heard a wise old woman say in her prayer, "Lord, fill my mouth with worthwhile stuff and nudge me when I've said enough." Sometimes we all need "nudging" from the Holy Spirit.

Prayer:

Father help me to tame my tongue that it may not be an unruly member of the body. I will keep my tongue from evil, and my lips from deceitful speech. Help me to be wise in my speech and my communications that I may not waver and be unstable. I put a watch over my thoughts today, and a guard over my lips that I may not sin with my mouth. I thank you, Lord, that you know how I should conduct myself, and how I should speak in season and out of season. May my words be seasoned with love, and my attitude be full of patience and grace. I desire to spread peace and not discord. I desire to edify and build up the body of Christ, and not tear down my Christian witness with words from my mouth. I am known by the fruit that I bear. Let joy be in my countenance, and may I respond to the Holy Spirit when He checks me whenever my flesh gets in the way. Forgive me for being a poor communicator and help me along the way to be one who edifies. Let my words be spoken with clarity to articulate the message of your kingdom, in Jesus' name. Amen.

Daily encouragement/Further scripture study and readings:

Monday: Colossians 4:6
Tuesday: 1 Peter 3:10
Wednesday: Ephesians 4:29
Thursday: Proverbs 10:19
Friday: James 3:8
Saturday: Matthew 5:37
Sunday: 1 Corinthians 15:33

A Rivaling Force

"Do nothing from rivalry or conceit, but in humility count others more significant than yourselves." Philippians 2:3 (NSV)

Weight/Sin: **Competitive Spirit**
(Aggressive, Ambitious, Rivalrous, Overzealous)

Inspiration:

A competitive spirit is an adversarial spirit of competition, a rivalry that sets one against another. Competition in the church puts saints at odds with one another. Someone will win and someone will lose. There is a spirit of competition that is seen among Christians when one wants to outdo, out preach, out minister, out sing, out pray, and even churches that want to outnumber another in membership. It is an enemy to the body of Christ, a trick of Satan to stir discord within the congregation. The root of this spirit is driven in envy, jealousy, and opposition. It will cause despair, tear down relationships, and destroy congregations.

We are many members in one body, with Christ as the head (1 Corinthians 12:12). The church is called to be in unity. There is no place for discord and competition. In the book of Acts 2:1, we read that the church was started and progressed because they were of one mind and of one accord. There was no competition. The Christian life is not a race of righteousness. It is not about you or me competing for a solitary prize, but it is about Jesus Christ. Competition can be healthy, or on the other hand, unhealthy. This journey for glory is not to the swift. It is not a pageant to display the popular. There is no gold medal to be the biggest, the best, the strongest, or fastest. There is no need for trying to outdo someone who seems to be successful in our eyes. Although, competition in the world especially, on the athletic level (it is the motivator for champions), is good and healthy, however, it is dangerous and very unhealthy in the church.

God is not the author of confusion. He does everything decently and in order. Competition will hinder and even stop the move of the Holy Spirit, because it is a rivaling force. It provokes a thirst for blind ambition. This deception opens a door to pride and arrogance. Competition will sidetrack the Christian and stop his progress in the work of the Lord. Then, he will fail to seek God's true plan for his life. Let us work diligently for the Lord. Let us seek and pursue the rewarder of righteous rewards and for spiritual and Godly gifts that only the Father can give. The race to run is the course that has been laid out by God when we came from our mother's womb. May our testimony be as Paul's, "I have run my race, fought a good fight, finished my course and kept the faith. Henceforth, there is laid up for me a crown of righteousness, which the Lord, the righteous judge, shall give me at the day of His coming; not me only but all that love His appearing" (2 Timothy 4:7–8).

Prayer:

Father, I thank you that this is not a race that I must finish first or be the best. If it were, I would surely lose. Forgive the competitive spirit that is found in me and in the Christian arena. Let me lay aside my evil ways and unite in one accord with the saints. Help me to labor while it is day, and to do all to the glory of God. Help me run this Christian race and be found righteous in your sight. I pray that the members in the body of Christ will began to work in one accord as the early church. As the Father, Jesus the Son, and the Holy Spirit are one, may we be one in you. I call in the power of agreement among all Christians and in our congregations. May we advance the kingdom of God one by one as we lay aside all competition in our attitudes and our lives across all denominational ministries. I thank you, Lord, for your healing waters flowing right now over my life and over the body of Believers, in Jesus name I pray. Amen.

Daily encouragement/Further scripture study and readings:

Monday: Hebrews 12:1
Tuesday: Philippians 2:3–4
Wednesday: Colossians 3:23
Thursday: Galatians 6:4
Friday: Ecclesiastes 2:22–26
Saturday: Ecclesiastes 9:11
Sunday: Matthew 19:30

You're Not the Boss of Me!

"Now, I beseech you, brethren, mark them which cause divisions and offenses contrary to the doctrine which ye have learned; and avoid them."
Romans 16:17

Weight/Sin: **Bossiness**
(Controlling, Domineering, Overbearing)

Inspiration:

We hear stories told of children growing up in a large family, and the older sibling is apt to lord over the younger, taking advantage of their size, their age, and gullibility. Then, one day, maturity is discovered in the younger, and he rebels with the cry "You're not the boss of me!" The revolt begins, and the bossiness of the elder comes to an end. There is mutiny in the camp until a truce is declared among the siblings. Usually, it is enforced by a higher authority, the parents. Bossiness is defined as overly authoritative. Bossiness and controlling people insist that you do what, how, and when they want; done their way *and* on their time schedule. Bossy and controlling people are self-absorbed, insensitive towards others, push to get their own way, and manipulate people and circumstances to achieve their own agenda.

"If anyone considers himself religious and does not bridle his tongue but deceives his own heart, this person's religion is worthless" (James 1:26, ESV). The person who dominates another lacks the capacity to enjoy a mature, loving relationship because he/she is consumed only with himself. They do not know how to love sacrificially for the benefit of others. This spirit of selfishness and self-centeredness, the bossy, controlling, demonic spirit is a spirit of witchcraft. Demonic manipulation is used to get people to do things they would not ordinarily do. This demonic enticement captures one's reasoning ability, forcing the manipulated to conform to wishes of the manipulator. Beware of a behavior that will manifest to the presence of a bossy, controlling, manipulative spirit. Whether you are the victim or perpetrator, God is able to break the cycles of this spirit.

We are no longer immature children. Paul wrote, "When I was a child, I spoke as a child, I understood as a child, I thought as a child; but when I became a man, I put away childish things" (1 Corinthians 1:11). With supervisors, managers, and business owners in the workplace, bossiness can only bring about resentment, but love will never fail to conqueror all malice. It is not for us to be domineering and bossy, but to treat people as we wish to be treated.

Prayer

Father God, in the name of Jesus Christ, I pray against these negative spirits of bossiness, including control, domination, and overbearing, and their powers to influence me. I cry out to you, God, for your help that these spirits have no jurisdiction to direct, or to sway, my behavior. In the name of Jesus and in the power of God, I take full authority, and I command this domineering spirit to flee according to the Word of God. Father, I seek you for deliverance. I have been controlled and manipulated by this spirit. God, it is your will that I am free of every stronghold and all demonic influences in my life. I come against every tethering cord, every attachment, and soul tie of this stronghold to this demonic force. God, I submit to you. I resist the devil, and your Word says that he will flee. In the name of Jesus and by the power of God, Satan, I rebuke you and your assignment against me is cancelled. I plead the blood of Jesus Christ to cover me, the power of God to protect me, and the fire of the Holy Spirit to burn up all the dross and impurities in my life.

I repent of all hidden, and unconfessed sins, lust of the flesh, lust of the eyes, and the pride of life. I reposition myself to be in your will.

I release and forgive anyone that I have held in unforgiveness. I close any door that I have opened to cause this spirit to come into my life. I renounce every word curse. God, your Word says that no weapon formed against me shall prosper, and every tongue that rises against me shall be found to be in the wrong. I am free of every stronghold! I praise God for deliverance! I will continue to be free. I am established in my place in the kingdom of God. I hide your Word in my heart that I may not sin against thee. I will study the Word to show myself approved unto you. I put on the whole armor of God. I will be fully equipped to stand against the wiles of the devil. Lord, I will trust you with all my heart and lean not to my own understanding. I will acknowledge you, and you shall direct my path. Lord, I declare that I am free from every controlling spirit in Jesus' name! Amen!

Daily encouragement /Further scripture study and readings:

Monday: James 4:7
Tuesday: Romans 16:17–18
Wednesday: Colossians 3:17
Thursday: Matthew 6:24
Friday: Luke 19:13
Saturday: Deuteronomy 8:18
Sunday: Romans 14:12
(Also, see overbearing, high-minded, insecurity)

Wrap Yourself in God's Security Blanket

"Be anxious for nothing but in everything by prayer and supplication with thanksgiving, let your requests be made known to God." Philippians 4:6 (NKJV)

Weight/Sin: **Insecurity**
(Insecure, Afraid, Unconfident, Anxious)

Inspiration:

Have you ever seen a toddler clinging to a small blanket, one that they want to carry everywhere they go? Sometimes the blanket is tattered and dingy; it certainly has seen better days. To them, the blanket carries a sense of security and familiarity. They are comforted when they have it. Just as the toddler, we all need to feel comforted and secure, regardless of our age. But sometimes we may lose our security and trust along the way. What happened? When people have been lied to, betrayed, hurt, and disappointed, they find it hard to put their trust in anyone or anything again. They even find it hard to believe the scriptures in the Word of God. Their faith wanes, and God becomes distant. They have lost their security. They become insecure. In the Word of God, it is written that when we are lost, we can find our way back into God's care. Reading the Word and believing what it says is like wrapping yourself in a security blanket that'll never be taken away from you.

An insecure person is fearful, they are not secure or confident in themselves, and they are always seeking validation from others. They are plagued by nervousness and anxiety. Inadvertently, these persons seek to impress others to receive validation and affirmation. They may attempt to drown out their reality with shopping, eating, promiscuity, drugs, or alcohol. We can only be secure in God. He is our protector. It's in Him that we are made whole, healed, and delivered. We are to seek to please God, and He alone validates us. Don't allow insecurity to make you feel as though God has forgotten or forsaken you.

God asks, "Can a woman forget her suckling child, and not have compassion on the son of her womb? Yes, they may but I will not forget thee." Now just wrap yourself in the "blanket" of security that only God can give! His word reminds us: "Do not fear, for I am with you; do not be dismayed, for I am your God. I will strengthen you and help you; I will uphold you with my righteous right hand" (Isaiah 41:10). The motto of a leading insurance firm is "Your car is in good hands" with their company. God has a better word for us than that insurance company. We are in the good hands of God. In fact, our names are engraved in the palm of his hand (Isaiah 49:16).

Prayer:

Father God, I am broken, fragmented, afraid, anxious, and insecure. I am on a trek of self-destruction through my insecurity. It is being magnified by cycles of fear and anxiety. I want to be free! I am not happy in this place. I have pretended long enough. I believe that through your shed blood, I can be free! Father God, my helper, my redeemer, I give all my insecurities to you that I might be healed. I cast every care upon you, for you care for me. You accept me just as I am. I rest in the security of your love for me. You have not given me the spirit of fear, insecurity, and anxiety, but of love, power, and a sound mind. I seek to please you, God, and you alone. Oh, do I love thee, Lord, my strength. You are my rock, and my deliverer. My strength in whom I trust. I am secure in you. In the name of Jesus Christ, my Lord. Amen!

LET IT ALL GO! WHAT ARE YOU "WEIGHTING" FOR?

Daily encouragement/Further scripture study and readings:

Monday: Philippians 4:6
Tuesday: 1 Peter 5:7
Wednesday: 2 Corinthians 10:12
Thursday: Romans 5:1–2
Friday: John 8:32
Saturday: Joshua 1:8–9
Sunday: John 15:7–8
(Also, see fear, anxiety, low self-esteem)

Encumbered About with Many Things

"But seek ye first the kingdom of God and His righteous, and all these things shall be added unto you." Matthew 6:33

Weight/Sin: **Stress**
(Pressure, Tension, Anxiety, Overtaxed)

Inspiration:

The sisters of Lazarus, Martha and Mary, were hosting a dinner party. They welcomed Jesus, His disciples, and other guests into their home. Martha cooked, served, and took care of the needs of their visitors. She was doing a good thing, but she was stressing herself out. She asked Jesus to send Mary to help her. Instead of Him sending her help, he rebuked Martha. Jesus said of Martha (Luke 10:38–42) that she was encumbered about with many things. She was busy, worrying and troubling herself with serving that she overlooked the thing that was needful: service in the Lord.

Mary was sitting at Jesus's feet relaxing, listening, and being fed with the Word. Her priority was to put the Lord first, and Jesus said that this would not be taken away from her. He was not going to send her away. It was up to her to rise and walk away, but she preferred to stay and listen. Martha was distracted by all the preparations that had to be made. She was pouring herself out in service, but not allowing the word to be poured back inside of her. In all her serving, she was neglecting her guest of honor, Jesus. He is the one who could strengthen her and put the joy back into her worship. The stressed-out person needs to stop and set some priorities, and do not allow their service to became void of devotion. Service apart from God is a thief and a robber. It will steal your joy, zap your strength, and encumber your relationship with the Lord.

It seems that we live in pursuit of happiness, but we've gotten caught up in the pursuit. We forget to put God first. A fact is our cup of what we want will never be full. And the saucer of what we do just keeps overflowing. Jesus said, "Seek ye first the kingdom of God and his righteousness and all these things shall be added unto you" (Matthew 6:33). He also reminded us that our heavenly Father takes care of the lilies of the field and the sparrows of the air, how much more will He take care of you and me (Luke 12::27–28, ASV). He knows what we need. It's time to release the stress from our lives and pursue what really matters. Choosing to put God first is a wise decision. When we reset our priorities and take time for God, the works that we do are constructive. In Christ, we will find grace for each day. He is our helper, burden bearer, strength, and peace. Where else can you gain such great peace? Jesus invites all who are worried and distracted by many things to sit and rest in His presence, to be renewed in faith and strengthen for service in the kingdom of God.

Prayer:

Father, in the name of Jesus, I repent of the stressful way I have handled many things. With all my serving, I have troubled myself to please the flesh. Flesh has no place in the kingdom of God. I ask you to forgive me and restore the joy I once had in my salvation. I recognize my faults, and I confess them. Bring peace to every area in my life that I may serve you in everything I say and do. Help me, Lord, that I may not fall back into a life of being overtaxed. May the Holy Spirit be my daily guide and lead me through the course of my day. I will keep my mind stayed on you as I seek to do your will. I thank you, that my heart shall overflow with joy, and my life shall be filled with goodness, as I rest in your presence. Amen.

Daily encouragement / Further scripture study and readings:

Monday: Luke 10:38–42
Tuesday: Psalm 37:7
Wednesday: Psalm 107:28–29
Thursday: Luke 12:27–28
Friday: Isaiah 9:6
Saturday: Matthew 16:24–26
Sunday: Romans 8:31
(Also, see anxiety, stress, busyness)

Can We Count on You?

"His Lord said unto him, well done, good and faithful servant; thou hast been faithful over a few things, I will make you ruler over many things: enter thou into the joy of thy Lord." Matthew 25:23

Weight/Sin: **Unfaithful**
(Untrustworthy, Inconsistent, Undependable)

Inspiration:

There are some people who look to have it all together, and maybe they do. They can handle work, household chores, their kids, lessons, pets, ball games, church services, activities, and so much more. But, do all the activities hinder their time with the Lord? Does it cause them to be unfaithful to their ministry and their calling? Will it cause them to be inconsistent with a devotional time in prayer? What keeps you out of church on Sunday morning, prayer meeting, and week night services? We find time to do other things, even sit and watch hours of television. Being unfaithful to God and the responsibilities in life will become evident and soon produce a fruitless life. I understand, we all have responsibilities that'll take us away from church. I understand that jobs sometime require us to miss church services, but what keeps us from sitting at the Lord's feet and being fed the Word? "Do not forsake the assembling ourselves together, (with believers), but exhorting one another; and so much the more as you see the day approaching" (Hebrews 10:25). We can find help and strength in Christian fellowship.

When I read Proverbs 31:10–30, of the virtuous woman, my first thought was she must be tired. Then I thought, she got it all together. She was faithful, industrious, and quite productive. She accomplished a lot during a twenty-four-hour period and was deemed virtuous. In all her deeds, she did not forget to clothe herself in strength and honor. She managed well her household, job, and family.

Notice also that she rose up early before daybreak. The verse concludes that a woman who fears the Lord shall be praised. She honored God, she feared the Lord, and her children called her blessed. With all her doings, she was found faithful, and she made time to make God her priority.

An unfaithful servant is so unreliable because they waver in life. A lifestyle such as that will not bear good fruit. It is a characteristic that is so undesirable that it is wicked to God. Jesus tells of the faithful and unfaithful servants in Matthew 25:18–30. The same were entrusted with a measure of talents. Two servants were faithful to use what they were given for their master's gain. One fearful servant, who is called unfaithful, did not recognize the value and potential of the talents he possessed. He disregarded the blessing that it could have been if he had put it to use. He was not faithful in the little, so, it was taken away from him. He lost it all. No business will prosper from an unfaithful employee, nor from one that leads an inconsistent, untrustworthy life. By the same scenario, so the church suffers as well. Jesus's teaches us to be faithful in our gifts and service. When we prove to be not trusted with a few assignments, then can we be trusted with more? Be faithful, saints, in the few things, and God will make you ruler over much. "We want God to say, 'Well done, good and faithful servant: thou hast been faithful over a few things, I will make thee ruler over many things: enter thou into the joy of the Lord." (Matthew 25:23).

Prayer

Father, I pray, that I may be found virtuous in your sight because a virtuous woman is priceless. I read that she considered your goodness and your promises and honored you. I fear and worship you, Lord. I set my love upon you. I desire to be diligent in the things of God. May my days be filled with meaningful tasks to accomplish what you want done. And may I use my talents for your glory that the blessings will last throughout all eternity. I ask for help in my daily responsibilities. Lead me by your Holy Spirit. Lead me in the paths that I must walk during my day. Lead me into righteousness. Teach me to number my days that I may apply my heart to wisdom. Wisdom is what I need and what I desire. I seek to redeem the times, for the days are evil. Help me walk with all circumspect and wisdom that I may know what the will of the Lord is for me. I place in your hands my pursuit for happiness, and I pursue an everlasting joy because I know that the joy of the Lord is my strength. Let my heart seek you early, and may my ways be found pleasing in your sight. In Jesus' name, I pray. Amen.

Daily encouragement/Further scripture study and readings:

Monday: Matthew 25:23
Tuesday: Ephesians 5:15–17
Wednesday: James 1: 8–22
Thursday: Proverbs 31: 10–30
Friday: Hebrews 10:23–25
Saturday: Chronicles 30:7
Sunday: Psalm 90:12

Pick Up the Pace

"The soul of the sluggard craves and gets nothing, while the soul of the diligent is richly supplied." Proverbs 13:4 (ESV)

Weight/Sin: **Slothful, Lazy**
(Idle, Sluggard, Lethargic)

Inspiration:

A sloth is a slow-moving mammal found in Central and South America that uses its long claws to hang upside down from tree branches. It is said that it sleeps fifteen to eighteen hours a day. He is slothful, idle, and he's usually asleep. He is not very exciting or the most sought-after animal. He is not like the enormous elephant, the tall giraffe, the beastly gorilla, or the kingly lion. He is not the favored animal of the zoo. Is he even in the zoo? We get a hearty laugh at the television commercial of a chubby boy laying on a couch with a TV remote in one hand and a cell phone in the other. The house phone rings, and you'll see in the background an elderly woman with the aid of a walker rushing, as much as she can, to answer the telephone. When she finally answers, it's the chubby boy lounging on the couch in front of the TV set asking grandma to bring him another soda. How sad!

Where is the energy that we once possessed? We must pick up the pace. A psychological study states that slothfulness is becoming a pandemic among young adults today because as children, they are not required to do chores in the home. So many of our children are not taught the importance of "work" or having household responsibilities. Some live between homes of divorced parents and, in many cases, grandparents. They are provided electronic gadgets and entertained with indoor comforts. Thus, we are enabling our children and producing a slothful generation. An old English proverb says: "Young and idle, old and needy." Idleness in youth makes way for a painful and miserable old age. Let us teach our children work ethics while they are young. Ecclesiastes 12:1 reads: "Remember now thy Creator in the days of thy youth."

Working while young will provide revenue for the future. A slothful person is called a sluggard. He is lethargic, idle, or lazy. He has a dislike for work or any kind of physical exertion. Proverbs 6:9–11 warns the slothful not to be young and idle, but to be useful and assiduous, or he will be poor and needy. There seems to be a lethargic spirit among the people of God. In God's business, we must be alert and diligent. All our efforts should be helpful in living the life that is well pleasing in the sight of God. In the Christian life, we all have a responsibility; we are ministers of reconciliation, and we are ambassadors in the kingdom of God (2 Corinthians 5:18–20).

Let our lives shine forth and be a witness that others may see our good works and glorify our Father which is in heaven. Let us be diligent, being doers of the Word and not hearers only. Let us be wise in winning souls to Christ. We do not know what tomorrow may bring, so work today while you are young, strong, vigilant, and in good health. There is no time for slackness. It is time to work while it is day, for nighttime comes when no man can work.

Prayer:

Heavenly Father, I repent for being idle and slothful in the things concerning God and my life. The time is drawing for the Lord's return, and I need to work for you like never before. I repent of my ways, and I ask you, Lord, for help in guiding me through every obstacle that may arise in my way. I am a minister carrying the words of eternal life that will reconcile man to God. What a responsibility! What an honor you have entrusted with me. Help me not be lazy and slow to do your will. I am an ambassador in your kingdom.

I will be alert to the Holy Spirit. I will be industrious and fruitful. I am strong, vigilant, and able to accomplish what you have set for me to do. I thank you, Father, in Jesus' name. Amen.

Daily encouragement / Further scripture study and readings:

Monday: Proverbs 20:4
Tuesday: Ephesians 5:16
Wednesday: Proverbs 19:15
Thursday: Matthew 25:26–30
Friday: Proverbs 6:9–11
Saturday: 2 Thessalonians 3:10–12
Sunday: Ecclesiastes 10:18

The Power of Life and Death Lies in the Tongue

"Death and life are in the power of the tongue."
Proverbs 18:21

Weight/Sin: **Meanness**
(Nastiness, Unkindness, Malicious, Hateful, Evil, Defaming)

Inspiration:

A mean-spirited person is unkind, cruel, have intentions to be hurtful, and they will rejoice when others fail. A mother of a child being bullied could not understand how some people can be so cruel. Bullying today has gone to a whole new level. It doesn't stop on the playground anymore or in the principal's office. It has gone viral! The toxic tongue has found new outlets to spew words of venom. Social media plays a big part in assisting in harassments. In this case, the cell phone was used to harass this child through text, video, Skype, Facebook, and Facebook Messenger-chat. It is called cyber bullying. Technology makes it convenient for the bullies to defame, harass, and even torment their victims to the point where the police get involved. We have even heard of fearful children committing suicide because of the hurt and the humiliation forced on them. We sometimes wonder where is God? Why did this happen to such an innocent child? Proverbs 15:3 lets us know: "The eyes of the Lord are in every place, beholding the evil and the good." He sees all Satan is doing. We do not live in a perfect world, but we do have a perfect Savior.

There are mean-spirited people who, for some reason, always seem angry. It is like they are confrontational, mean-spirited, sarcastic, and looking for a fight all the time. Their tongues are toxic, and their words bite like a viper. They speak unkind words of venom; words that can pierce the spirit of the listener, (see weight on *hurt*). It is as if they do not know how to be kind. I once read a quote that stated: "Some people are just mean. Don't take it personally, it says nothing about you, but it speaks volumes about them." In 1 Kings chapters 9–12, we read in this story of such a woman, Queen Jezebel, an evil woman who was the wife of King Ahab. She exalted herself and placed her meanness on public display. Her behavior expressed in her words and deeds created an environment of hate and an atmosphere that was full of maliciousness. Meanness is such ungodly behavior, especially when we are charged to be kind and loving. We may not think of it as sinful, and a mean person may not see themselves as such; but to others, they are offensive.

I have been the victim of a mean, toxic tongue, just as you may have been. The sadness of the situation is that the person was a Christian. I had to remind myself of the word that reads in Luke 6:28, "Bless them that curse you, and pray for them which despitefully use you." Don't let meanness dominate your tongue, your attitude, or your behavior. We are being observed by an unbelieving world to see if we are genuine and true to the Word. We must bridle our tongues, watch our actions, and not put our attitudes on public display. Don't let meanness cause the people you love to avoid you and reject Jesus. Let us conduct ourselves in a Christ-like manner speaking those things that are pure, true, and of a good report. Proverbs 15:4 says, "A wholesome tongue is a tree of life: but perverseness is a breach in the spirit." Let us bless people and not curse them, not be the cause of harm or trouble. We are to bless the people that they may become a blessing in service to God.

Prayer:

Father, I may not recognize how I sound or come across to others, but I repent of being mean and for having a toxic tongue. I ask that your Holy Spirit come and cleanse my soul from all sin. Help me to find the root cause of my meanness and nasty attitude. Reveal to me the hidden pains in my own heart. Heal me of all the hurts and disappointments I hid in my life. Search me Lord, search me through and through. Forgive me for any pain I may have caused someone. I read Psalm 1:1, as a confession over my life. I will not walk in the ways of the ungodly, nor be accused of standing in the way of sinners, nor sit on the seat of the scornful. But I will find delight in your Word and meditate on it day and night. I will be like the tree that is planted by the waters of God that will flourish and bear fruit, and, my tongue shall be a wholesome tree of life, in Jesus' name I pray. Amen.

Daily encouragement /Further scripture study and readings:

Monday: Matthew 5:40
Tuesday: 1 Peter 3:4, 15
Wednesday Galatians 3:28
Thursday: John 19:11
Friday: Romans 8:9
Saturday: Titus 3:1–5
Sunday: Philippians 2:3
(also, see hurt, intimidation)

Consider the Ant

"Come unto Me, all you who are weary and burdened, and I will give you rest."
Matthew 11:28 (NIV)

Weight/Sin: **Overly Committed**
(Overzealous, Driven, Severely Obligated)

Inspiration:

    One day, I was observing a gathering of ants that covered a small piece of bread. One by one, each ant would break away from the crowd, carrying off a crumb back to their colony. The group seemed so very busy as they whittled away at the bread. They looked as if they were scattered, hurried about, full of activity. Although they were rushing as a team about seemingly in all directions, I know by what I had been taught about ants, they were working collectively. In no time, the bread was gone, and they accomplished their task! My mind quickly turned to the hustle and bustle of our everyday lives. We live in a very busy world and a fast-paced society.
    People are always on the go. We are on the move from the time the alarm clock goes off until the end of the day. We don't seem to stop until we go to bed at night. We're not necessarily rushing around meaninglessly, or mismanaging our time, but we are getting into situations of being overly committed. We have too many responsibilities, whether they are voluntary or involuntary. We've over committed ourselves in the workplace, home, family, friends, activities, entertainment, hobbies, and even church and its related services. Sometimes, our day gets so hectic that we see that we have too many

"irons in the fire," and they all demand our attention. There are just not enough hours in the day because we are spreading ourselves way too thin. Then we get stressed out with all the good that we do in serving.

Jesus is calling out to the weary: "Come unto me all you that labor and are heavy laden and I will give thee rest. Take my yoke upon you and learn of me; for I am meek and lowly in heart; and you shall find rest for your souls for my yoke is easy and my burden light" (Matthew 11: 28–30). Consider the ant, child of God, in all his doings he remained focused, diligent, and committed. He carefully planned what was priority. The ants accomplished their task, and it benefited the whole colony. Being overly committed, no matter how spirited, if it's aimless and meaningless, it bears no fruit. What good is it if nothing of virtue is accomplished? Commitments led by the spirit of God will set things in order in a virtuous way, and then, it will bear eternal fruit. Jesus knew we'd need Him in our everyday activities. "Come unto me," He calls, "and I will give you rest." We need to seek Him daily to find rest for our soul.

Prayer:

Father, in the name of Jesus, I thank you for being my Father, my strength when I am weak, and my strong arm when I am falling. Forgive me, Lord, when I spread myself too thin. I feel like I am going in all directions. I have overly committed myself, and I don't seem to have enough time to get alone and pray.

I decided that I will seek you first and spend time in your presence. I will consider my ways. I willfully bow, surrender, and submit all areas of my life to you. Help me to be focused and commit only to what I am able to do. Help me to manage my time and not overload my day. I desire to worship you, sit at your feet, and I know I'll be blessed. I pray that my enthusiasm in serving will be turned toward you and the church. Let me be diligent in my ways that you may be glorified. Father, I thank you now because I am believing you for a modest demeanor in my responsibilities, in Jesus' name. Amen.

Daily encouragement /Further scripture study and readings:

Monday: I Timothy 5:6
Tuesday: Colossians 3:23–24
Wednesday: Galatians 6:9
Thursday: Psalm 128:2
Friday: Proverbs 23:4
Saturday: 1 John 2:17
Sunday: Ecclesiastes 3:1
(also see busyness, stress)

From a Promiscuous Past to a Faithful Future

"I beseech you therefore brethren by the mercies of God that ye present your bodies a living sacrifice holy acceptable unto God which is your reasonable service. And be not conformed to this world but be ye transformed by the renewing of your mind, that ye may prove what is that good and acceptable and perfect will of God."
Romans 12:1–2

Weight/Sin: **Infidelity**
(Unfaithfulness, Wantonness, Adultery, Deceitfulness)

Inspiration:

    Infidelity, adultery, fornication, sexual immorality; these are subjects we tend to avoid because one can be looked upon as being a prude and sanctimonious. Fidelity is a pure and normal behavior according to the Word of God. Our society has made infidelity a desirable lifestyle, it is publicized in movies, television, and celebrity publications. This portrayal has become a poor role model for the impressionable. It is treated as normal behavior in the world, and has even been found and exposed in the church. However, we know that sexual immorality violates God's standards for living, it is not Christlike behavior, and it is addressed in 1 Corinthians 6:12–20. Infidelity is a damaging sin. Not only do you sin against God and your spouse, but you sin against your own body as well!

I was listening to a pastor's panel as they answered questions from the audience. A young woman wanted to know if she was in sin for having a sexual relationship with a married man. She argued the fact that *she* was not the married one; therefore, he was the adulterer and the sinner. She wanted to continue in the relationship. See how she is deceived and blinded to the truth? Sexual sin is in no way right in the eyes of God! God made it clear that marriage is honorable, a holy union. "Let marriage be held in honor among all, and let the marriage bed be undefiled, for God will judge the sexually immoral and adulterous" Hebrews 13:4 (ESV). You are joined to your spouse by law to forsake all others. Those who have entered a marital relationship are to be true and faithful in their marriage, and those who are not married, are to be celibate.

Romans 12:1–2 reads: "I beseech you therefore brethren by the mercies of God that ye present your bodies a living sacrifice, holy, acceptable unto God, which is your reasonable service. And be not conformed to this world: but be ye transformed by the renewing of your mind, that ye may prove what is that good, and acceptable, and perfect will of God". The bible tells us to "flee from sexual immortality. Every other sin a person commits outside the body, but the sexually immoral person sins against his own body. Do you not know that your body is the temple of the Holy Spirit within you, whom you received from God? You are not your own, you are bought with a price. So, glorify God in your body" I Corinthians 6:18–20 (ESV).

Submit to God and resist temptation! Decide today and be determined to commit your ways unto God, and Satan will flee. God has good, acceptable, and perfect plans for your life. He wants you to live honorably and obediently as a living sacrifice for his service. "Know ye not that you are the temple of the Holy Ghost?" As a living sacrifice, repent and present your body to God. You will find that our God is a good Father, waiting for you with His arms open wide. He stands at the door of your heart, and He knocks. If you open, He will come in and dwell with you. He will forgive you and restore peace back into your life. Although you may have had a promiscuous past, our Father has for you a faithful future.

Prayer:

Heavenly Father, oh, how I repent for the sexual sins in my life. Forgive my dishonesty. Dear God, cleanse my heart, cleanse my mind. Let me be cleansed from all secret faults and sins. May my life be free from infidelity and the shame that is associated with it. I see the damage it has caused in my life and the lives of others. Help me to resist temptation. Help me recognize snares and traps that will cause me to stumble. Let me hide myself in thee.

I present my body a living sacrifice unto you! I am a temple of the Holy Ghost. I want to be whole again. I choose this day to walk in the light, and not in darkness. I present myself as a consecrated vessel to be used in your service. There is a work for me to do. I desire to minister in whatever area you have designed for me. Lord, may I honor you in all I say and do. I pray these things in Jesus' name. Amen.

Daily encouragement /Further scripture study and readings:

Monday: Isaiah 29:15
Tuesday: Proverbs 5:1–7
Wednesday: Proverbs 6:24–26
Thursday: Galatians 5:19–21
Friday: Romans 12:1–2
Saturday: 1 Corinthians 6:12–20
Sunday: Hebrews 13:4–8

Transformed from Passive to Passionate

"Create in me a clean heart, O God, and renew a right spirit within me." Psalm 51:10

Weight/Sin: **Apathy**
(Apathetic Passiveness, Detachment, Insensitivity)

Inspiration:

    I have watched reality television shows that portray people with a passion for life, who travel to remote places to survive in extreme conditions; another shows traveling all over the world to eat the strangest cuisine and delicacies of that culture. It seems they exist to awake and arise for their next challenge. The church does not seem to be or even want to be challenged anymore. We have become comfortable and apathetic. We have a form of godliness but deny the power thereof (2 Timothy 3:5).
    Apathy is a state of mind and reflecting attitude where a person shows little or no interest, concern, passion, emotion, or excitement. This failure to engage is exhibited by a spirit of prayerlessness. Apathy is detachment and insensitivity and causes problems in every area of life and relationship. This unconcerned passiveness is detrimental, naturally, and spiritually. As spiritually and emotionally healthy beings, it is our nature to show concern, interest, sensitivity, passion, and compassion. God can heal and restore peace, love, and hope in our lives through His power and through His love for us. Today, I believe there is a wake-up call vibrating through the body of

Christ because of the transformation that is taking place. There is an awakening of the church from passive to passionate. The church is being transformed from the passive, apathetic state of existence to a powerful place of precision.

The church must be the authority on the earth, rising to the challenge to take on and take back the things of God from Satan's crowd and having the existence of Godliness with the power to back it up! No longer accepting or allowing what happens or what others do, without an active response or resistance. It is not God's way. Passive is the opposite of active. God has instructed us to display our works: faith without works is dead. Someone who is passive tends to accept anything that comes their way, including what others might say, without any action or response, even when they know that it is in error. They tend to be detached and insensitive to what is happening around them, and they show little to no interest in making things better. When we seek God and ask Him to lead us and guide us in everything, we always have a course of action! Let the Lord lead you to take a stand for the truth. Take everything to the Lord in prayer!

Prayer:

Father, God, I come against apathy in my life. I pray for restoration of passion and enthusiasm for life and ministry. I have a renewed mind. I am not conformed to this world, but I am transformed by the renewing of my mind. My mind is renewed by the power of the Holy Spirit. I study the Word of God; I hide the scriptures in my heart. Revelation 3:8a,16, tells me that you know my works, and you would prefer me to be either hot or cold, for when I am lukewarm, I am spewed out of your mouth! According to Romans 12:9–13, I pray that my love be genuine. That I abhor what is evil and hold fast to what is good; loving one another with brotherly affection, outdoing one another in showing honor, that I am not slothful in zeal but fervent in spirit, serving you, Lord. I rejoice in hope, am patient in tribulation, constant in prayer, and contribute to the needs of others showing hospitality. I am caring and compassionate. Restore to me the joy of your salvation and uphold me with a willing spirit. Passion is restored in me, in Jesus' name. Amen.

Daily encouragement/Further scripture study and readings:

Monday: Hebrews 5:11–12
Tuesday: Ephesians 5:16
Wednesday: John 5:39–40
Thursday: Mark 14:38–41
Friday: James 4:17
Saturday: Hebrews 11:6
Sunday: Revelation 3:16

For Thirty Pieces of Silver

"Yea, mine own familiar friend, in whom I trusted, which did eat of my bread, hath lifted up his heel against me." Psalm 41:9

Weight/Sin: **Betrayal**
(Deception, Treachery, Disloyalty)

Inspiration:

Betrayal, deception, and trickery seem to make fodder for movie story plots. These actions capture the viewers and keep them in suspense throughout the movie. "*Et tu, Brute?*" These are the infamous last words of Julius Caesar as he looked into the face of his betrayer, Marcus Brutus. Those words mean, "Even you, Brutus?" It was a surprise to Caesar to see his confidant among the assassins. He knew about the conspiracy of the other statesmen, but not Brutus. "Et tu, Brute?" You too, my confidant? My comrade? My friend who has become my traitor.

Judas Iscariot greeted the Master with a kiss. It was the telltale sign he gave the guards to act fast and arrest Jesus. Jesus too looked into the face of his betrayer and spoke, "Judas, betray thou the Son of man with a kiss" (Luke 22:48). Jesus knew that Judas would betray him, but to kiss him first? It was not a gesture of love or affection, but a deceptive, disloyal kiss. He conspired with the chief priests and Pharisees and betrayed the King of glory! Betrayal is an act of deliberate disloyalty. It is an intentional offense that is misleading and deceitful. It reflects one's heart and character and shows a lack of integrity. For thirty pieces of silver, Judas Iscariot betrayed Jesus (see Matthew 26:14–16). Betrayal is to take advantage of an intimate relationship by breaking trust and destroying the faith. Infidelity is betrayal in marriage. Gossiping is betrayal in friendship. Lying, cheating, and stealing are all forms of betrayal as well. Violating fiduciary responsibility in business issues is also an act of betrayal. Victim or perpetrator, betrayal destroys trust and violates confidence; it is a strong offense.

Betrayal is a deliberate, hurtful action, generally portrayed upon someone with whom there is a relationship. You come not to expect any real loyalty from strangers, but when the betrayal is within your "'camp," it really hurts! Because of Jesus' exemplary response to ultimate betrayal, as the ones closest to Him betrayed Him, we too can move past the hurt and find wholeness again! "No temptation has overtaken you that is common to man: God is faithful, and He will not let you be tempted beyond your ability, but with the temptation, He will also provide a way of escape, that you may be able to endure" (1 Corinthians 10:13). Look for that escape. God's promise of escape is a promise of trust. Trust in Him! He alone can move you beyond the hurt to wholeness again.

Prayer:

Father, your word says, "Blessed is the man who remains steadfast under trial, for when he has stood the test, he will receive the crown of life, which God has promised to those who love Him" (James 1:12, ESV). Lord, I come to you hurting from my betraying ways, as I see the hurt that I have caused. No one wins! I pray the weight of betrayal is never again associated with me, as I have experienced, firsthand, the deep hurt that this deception brings. Lord, I pray for those who have been hurt by the disloyalty of my words and deeds. Lord, I remain steadfast. I'll not succumb under this trial. I will neither stop nor become weary in doing your will. According to your Word in Isaiah 54:17 (ESV), "No weapon fashioned against you shall succeed, and you shall refute every tongue that rises against you in judgment." This is my heritage and vindication from you. I will continue to fight the good fight of faith and encourage myself in you, Lord. I choose to forgive as you have forgiven me.

Daily encouragement /Further scripture study and readings

> Monday: Proverbs 19:5
> Tuesday: Genesis 12:3
> Wednesday: Matthew 24:10
> Thursday: Jeremiah 12:6
> Friday: Judges 16:15
> Saturday: Mark 11:25
> Sunday: Psalm 109:4

You Can Run, But You Can't Hide

"The impurities of the wicked ensnare him, and he is held fast in the cords of his sin."
Proverbs 5:22 (ESV)

Weight/Sin: **Addictions**
(Dependency, Fetish, Obsession)

Inspiration:

Christians have come to me and asked, "Is drinking alcoholic beverages wrong? Is smoking wrong? Participating in sociable "partying?" "Indecent Internet viewing? Private partying? Are these sinning?" My answer was this: If you had to ask, then it is wrong! Because, apparently, the Holy Spirit is doing His job by convicting you of sin and dealing with you by grieving the Holy Spirit within you.

Sin in any form is a bad witness and very damaging to the Christian character. Addiction is not just in reference to drugs, alcohol, and gambling. An addiction is anything that enslaves us. It can be alcohol, illicit or prescription drugs, sex, pornography, cigarettes, foods, sugar, coffee, soda, electronic devices, gaming, television, shopping, shoes, clothing, murmuring and complaining, gossiping, negative talk, critical mind sets or *anything else* that you feel that you cannot live without; but causes harm, wasting and consuming your time, your health, and your resources, preventing you from moving forward and living a full God ordained life. Addictions hinder you from pursuing His purpose for your life.

Addictions are habits, cravings, and appetites that cause dependency and obsession. Addictions can be broken through the power of God. It is not the will of our Father God for any to be controlled by fleshly cravings of any addiction; whether chemical, physical, or of mind, body, will, or emotions. Addictions can cause financial drain, illness, destroy relationships, marriages and families, can lead to imprisonment, and even death. Don't be guilty of addictive behaviors. Many people confessing to be Christians are being found to harbor secret sins. God is aware of all our secrets; nothing is hidden from Him. Psalm 90:8 says, "Thou hast set our iniquities before thee, our secret sins in the light of thy countenance." God already knows all our secrets, and He will forgive us if we would only confess them and ask for forgiveness. Be careful, my dear friend, your sins will find you out (Numbers 32:23). What is done behind closed doors, in the privacy of your own home, may be your own business, but it is also God's business. What is hidden and done in the darkness will sooner or later come to light (Luke 8:17).

It is time for Christians to deal with their undercover habits and the secret sins in their lives. Sin in any form is a bad witness and very damaging to the Christian character. What may have started as a willful small act can lead to a habit, then an addiction. The good news is that God will forgive us of our sins. "Do you not know that if you present yourselves to anyone (or anything) as obedient slaves, you are slaves of the one whom you obey, either of sin, which leads to death, or of obedience, which leads to righteous?" (Romans 6:16 ESV). Won't you confess now and allow God to break the chains of bondage, and once again allow God to rule supreme and Lord over your life? The power of prayer and reading of the scriptures will provide insight and support in your decision to be free of ungodly addictions. This is a declaration of your faith and the start of a closer relationship with God. Healing, deliverance, and restoration is available through the power of God's Word! Whether seeking deliverance for yourself or for someone else, trust God. He can deliver and set free!

Prayer:

Father, God, I cry out for your help. I have an addiction to (confess addiction). Thank you for the desire to be free and to no longer be enslaved by addictions. God, your Word says, "For freedom, Christ has set us free; stand firm, therefore, and do not submit again to a yoke of slavery."

Father, I pray against every demonic stronghold of this addiction. I submit to you, God. I resist the evil temptation of this addiction, and it flees from me. I am persistent in standing in faith for healing and deliverance; that I am no longer enslaved and obedient to cravings and the mind-set of serving my flesh. I am obedient to you, God. According to Romans 12:1, Lord, by your mercies, I present my body as a living sacrifice, holy and acceptable to God, which is reasonable service. God, your word promises that no temptation has overtaken me that is not common to man. God, you are faithful, and will not let me be tempted beyond my ability, but with the temptation, you will also provide the way of escape, that I may be able to endure it (1 Corinthians 10:13). As I walk free of addiction, I pray for strength to remain addiction-free. I will refrain from bad company. I will not be deceived as your Word says, "Do not be deceived: bad company ruins good morals" (I Corinthians 15:33 ESV). I stand in faith and walk in deliverance in the name of Jesus. Amen!

(pray this prayer for yourself or someone else)

Daily encouragement/Further scripture study and readings:

Monday: Proverbs 23:20–21a
Tuesday: Proverbs 20:1
Wednesday: Ephesians 5:18–20
Thursday: Colossians 3:5
Friday: Galatians 5:19–21
Saturday: Hebrews 13:4
Sunday: 2 Corinthians 5:17

God's Anger Management Program

"Be angry, but sin not." Ephesians 4:26a

Weight/Sin: **Anger**
(Rage, Irate, Indignation, Wrath, Aggravation)

Inspiration:

Take a deep breath. Count to ten. Go for a walk. Take a time out. These are tips offered by the "experts" to suppress angry outbursts. The best kind of management of anger is the kind that helps to channel feelings appropriately rather than bottling them up. Having the feelings of anger is not the problem: it's what we do with them. We all have heard and read about road rage, domestic violence, perpetrators of hate and other violent crimes, and the list goes on and on. We think, *how cruel, what a shame,* but we never hear of anyone doing much of anything about the root causes of the problems. Everyone doing their part to make this world a "kinder, gentler place" seems to be a forgone reality.

Several years ago, we were bombarded by advertisements introducing free classes on anger management. Schools adopted programs into their curricular to help students with social emotional issues associated with managing their anger. Parents of preschoolers to high schoolers were involved in parenting classes to help them with issues involving the upbringing of their children. Large corporations adapted their programs and required their employees to participate in the courses. The counselors taught on the causes of anger, stress debriefing, and relaxation techniques. People don't think of anger as a sin because it doesn't seem to be a *"big sin"* like breaking one of the Ten Commandments. But unrestrained anger is a sin. It can be seen in a child throwing a tantrum to uncontrolled behavior in fury.

Jesus taught on anger in Matthew 5:22. A suppressed anger held within will cause resentment, jealousy, bitterness, and irritability. Uncontrolled anger harbors strife, discord, and violence. As in road rage, it can blow up to be volatile, even committing murder. Control your anger! Get a hold on your thoughts. Whatever happened to the "take five" to calm down? Or stop and count to ten? In the book of Ephesians, chapter 4 verse 26 tells us to be angry, but sin not. Do not let the sun go down and you're still angry. Call out to God and vent your frustrations and allow the Lord to bring in a peace in the midst of all that angers you. We are not a people of darkness, little children, but we are children of the light. We must learn to manage our anger. Don't subscribe to the notion of "destruction therapy," as it has been called when physical aggression and hostility are used as a release mechanism for anger emotions. *Let it all go!* Let us put away strife and malice and refuse to allow Satan to use us to participate in rage, volcanic outbursts or other ways of destroying one another.

Releasing anger in destructive ways or holding anger on the inside, either of these habits can lead to more destruction. These emotions distract from God's plan for your life to live peacefully with one another. There is a rightful place for anger having a holy indignation to see justice and righteousness prevail! Let us begin by turning our hearts and minds toward Christ, and operate in love, ministering forgiveness and speaking peace to our fellowman. The Word of God says, "We wrestle not with flesh and blood, but with principalities, rulers of darkness, and wickedness in high places." It is not people we should fight and war against, but Satan. He is the evil one. He is the thief that comes only to steal, kill, and destroy our life in Christ. Resist the devil, and he will flee from you! Don't give in to these emotions of anger; they will keep us out of the race to eternal life!

Prayer:

Father, the anger I feel inside of me has hindered my work with others. I have walked away and avoided people because I have been angry with them. Lord, I chose to lay aside this weight of anger that has attempted to keep me bound. I release these feelings to you. I forgive everyone that has wronged me that I may be forgiven. Help me to live peacefully with all men. Bring peace to my life as I minister peace to all I meet. I pray that I can join with other Christians and work in a ministry that edifies and doesn't tear down the body of Christ. Lord, you have blessed me. I am an overcomer, by the blood of the Lamb and by the words of my testimony. I thank you, Lord, that you have deemed me worthy to be your child. I thank you that anger has no dominion over me. It is under my feet. I am the righteousness of God in Christ Jesus! In Jesus' name I pray. Amen.

Daily encouragement /Further scripture study and readings:

Monday: Psalm 37:8–9
Tuesday: Ephesians 4:26–31
Wednesday: Proverbs 15:1, 18
Thursday: Colossians 3:8
Friday: James 1:19–20
Saturday: Psalm 43:5
Sunday: Matthew 11:28

The Green-Eyed Monster

"For where jealousy and selfish ambition exist there will be disorder and every vile practice." James 3:16 (ESV)

Weight/Sin: **Jealousy**
(Envy, Covetousness, Resentment, Suspicion)

Inspiration:

It is easy for us to become jealous of someone even when our intentions are good. God tells us that He is a jealous God! He wants us to exclusively serve Him, much like a husband who will guard his wife from another man's affections. Jealousy can be right and appropriate, but it also can be dangerous when it becomes an obsession. The Bible tells us in the Song of Solomon 8:5 that "jealousy is cruel as the grave." Jealousy can creep into our lives in numerous ways. Once we become aware of the weight/sin, we must approach it with confession, prayer, and scripture. We must rule over it and not let it rule over us!

As evident in the story of brothers Cain and Able, Cain allowed jealousy to take root in his heart. In this biblical account, God showed favor upon Abel's sacrifice; because it was an offering from the best that he had to give. Cain allowed jealousy to enter his heart towards his brother and became angry and enraged towards him. As jealousy turned to hatred, Cain lured his brother into a field and killed him, ostensibly out of a jealous rage! (Read entire account in Genesis 4:1–16).

LET IT ALL GO! WHAT ARE YOU "WEIGHTING" FOR?

I Corinthians 3:3 (ESV) says, "For you are still in the flesh. For while there is jealous and strife among you, are you not of the flesh and behaving only in a human way? Therefore, since we know that we have a sinful nature, we must consciously "lay aside every weight and sin that can so easily beset us!" Let it go!

Beauty pageants for little girls, oh, how cute! We can be sure that the toddlers, as well as the adult women in these competitions, are coached to present themselves in an elegance that the judges are looking for and expecting. The presentation in their smile and ladylike mannerisms does not tell what goes on backstage. I would like to think that the competitions are proper and wholesome, but knowing the nature of girls, I know better. Behind the curtains and lurking in the shadows, beneath the makeup, the pretty dresses, and the tiaras is the green-eyed monster—jealousy. It is the effect of man's sinful nature.

Selfish gain is a manipulating evil that roams about, seeking to inflict an individual with suspicious thoughts, envy, and all that's associated with jealousy. How often have we experienced jealousy; to envy someone who has received recognition from peers, to desire a position someone else holds, to dislike a person who just seems to have it all? We must immediately dismiss these thoughts! We cannot let this evil dominate in our lives. Jealousy is a rival with the Spirit of God. It can cause destructive emotions and destructive behaviors. Look at the lives of Cain and Abel, Jacob and Esau, Leah and Rachel, Joseph and his brothers, Saul and David in the Bible. If they were alive today, they could all testify of the evils of jealousy. Take an honest look at yourself. Let the Holy Spirit reveal what's inside of you.

Acknowledge jealousy, envy, and any ulterior motive that is found in you. Confess it to the Lord. Bring it under subjection with the Word of God. The Lord will meet your need and empower your life. He will create inside of you a clean heart and renew the right spirit within you. Seek the Lord while He may be found and desire a hunger and thirst for His righteousness. Be diligent concerning your salvation and contend for the faith. It is God's will for you to grow into spiritual maturity. Although God rebukes and corrects man and it seems you can't bear the test, He will restore you, and you will see that your ways are full of vanity. Let your hands be clean and your heart pure. Go before the Lord with thanksgiving and praise. Worship the Lord in the beauty of His holiness.

Prayer:

Father, in the name of Jesus, I am as a leper of old, needing to be cleansed and healed. I will take heed of your Word and mark my ways. I call on the name of the Lord because my hope is in you. I ask to be forgiven for the ulterior motives I have hidden hoping no one can see them. Deliver me from all my transgressions. I repent of a jealous heart and my suspicious behavior. I release to you all my self-proclaimed ambitions. I ask for your will to be done in my life. Lord, I need your Holy Spirit to renew the right spirit within me. Help me to recognize Satan as the enemy when he comes and tries to overtake me. Grant me grace and mercy to have the strength to resist the enemy. I place myself in your hands. I am solely thine. Teach me your ways, Lord and separate me from the wicked. I know that I am yours, and I commit my ways to you. I desire your will and your way for my life. I am running after you, Lord, with my whole heart. Take over my mind, my heart, and my desires. Make me to know you again and I shall rejoice in victory. Amen.

Daily encouragement /Further scripture study and readings:

Monday: Job 5:2
Tuesday: James 3:14–16, 4:2–3
Wednesday: Proverbs 14:30, 27:4
Thursday: Luke 15:25–30
Friday: I Corinthians 3:3
Saturday: Corinthians 11:2
Sunday: Romans 12:21

Sticks and Stones Break Bones, and Words Can Hurt You Too!

"He heals the brokenhearted and binds up their wounds." Psalm 147:3 (NIV)

Weight/Sin: **Hurt**
(Wounded, Abused, Suffering, Sorrow)

Inspiration:

Do you remember the childhood saying, "Sticks and stones may break my bones, but words will never hurt me"? The truth of the matter is that words do hurt. Hurtful words can wound the heart, the spirit, and the soul, leaving a heap of damaged people. Proverbs 18:21 states that there is death and life in the power of the tongue. Negative accusations, critical words, and gossip can cut and wound the heart, cutting like a dagger while penetrating the spirit and wounding the heart. The heart is crushed, and the spirit is bruised. It is like a very painful wound that seemingly won't heal. It is as if you've been knocked off your feet, and you can't get up. When the heart hurts and the spirit is bruised, it is hard to be bold in the things of God and move out in the spirit. Many have found (what the word of God teaches) that doctors can not heal a wounded spirit. But there is good news! What doctors cannot do; God has already done through the finished work of Jesus Christ. Jesus came to heal the broken hearted and set the captive free.

Jeremiah 17:14 reads, "Heal me, O Lord, and I shall be healed; save me, and I shall be saved: for thou art my praise." He suffered and died for our emotional pains as well! Jesus saved us to walk in freedom. The Lord's prayer teaches us to pray and ask our heavenly Father to forgive us our trespasses as we forgive those who trespass against us. As we release our faith through genuine repentance, we can receive our healing. Freedom is what the Christian faith is all about: the freedom that we have in Christ Jesus. Hurtful feelings, wounded and bruised emotions, are a few of the enemy's tactics to separate us from God's love. The Word tells us in Romans 8:35–38, "Who can separate us from the love of Christ? Shall tribulation, or distress, persecution, famine, nakedness, peril or sword? Nay, we are more than conquerors through Him that loved us. I am persuaded that neither death, life, angels nor principalities, nor powers, nor things present nor things to come, nor depth, height or any other creature shall be able to separate us from the love of God which is in Christ Jesus our Lord."

God doesn't pull away, but Satan wants us to pull back. We try and convince ourselves that it is to protect ourselves and our loved ones from further pain. I thank the Lord that He doesn't leave us alone. The Holy Spirit brings comfort and restores our joy. It may have been a long time since you've felt the presence of the Lord. So, forgive those who have spitefully treated you and accept and receive your miracle. "Blessed are you when others revile against you and persecute you and utter all kinds of evil against you falsely on my account. Rejoice and be glad for your reward is great in heaven" Matthew 5:11–12 (ESV). God has blessings in store for you. The good work that God has started in you, He is faithful to complete it.

Prayer:

Father, In the name of Jesus, I have been hurt and utterly wounded. I have hidden myself away from others to avoid being hurt again. This is such a lonely place. I see no spiritual growth, and you want me to grow in the things of God. I forgive everyone that has come against me and hurt me in any way. I ask you to pour into me the oil and the wine, for my healing of this hurt, may it flow to every wound and hurting place, healing me from the inside out. Fill me up with your spirit. I want more of you, more of your Word, and more of your love. Help me, Lord, that I may love those who come against me, that your love shown in me, may turn their hearts back to you. I thank you that I am anointed of you. Help me to always use my words to heal and not hurt when conversing with others. I am called in these last days to do a mighty work in the kingdom of God. He who wins souls is wise. Help me to lead someone to Christ today. In Jesus's name I ask and pray. Amen.

Daily encouragement /Further scripture study and readings:

Monday: Genesis 26:29
Tuesday: Psalm 15:4, 109:22
Wednesday: Proverbs 18:6, 18:8, 18:14
Thursday: Isaiah 53:5
Friday: Jeremiah 10:19
Saturday: Romans 8:18, 8:35–39
Sunday: 1 Peter 5:1

Forgive Seventy Times Seven

"For if ye forgive men their trespasses, your Heavenly Father will also forgive you." Matthew 6:14

Weight/Sin: **Unforgiving**
(Unyielding, Uncharitable, Hardhearted, Bitterness, Stubborn)

Inspiration:

Peter asked Jesus, "How many times should we forgive a person that has wronged us? Seven times?" Jesus responded, we are to forgive everyone as many as seventy-times-seven times; which equals four-hundred and ninety times. Looking at this number; it seems impossible for one person to offend another that many times in a lifetime. Could this be the logic behind the statement Christ made and the number four-hundred and ninety? Yes, because the number symbolizes boundlessness.

I attended a service and heard a testimony of a preacher and his wife as they shared their story of wrestling with forgiveness. Their daughter was killed in a car accident by a young man in a drunken stupor. He was tried, convicted, and sent to prison. This preacher headed a prison ministry at the same facility where this young man was imprisoned. He wanted to quit the ministry, change facilities, and / or delegate the ministry to someone else. After many spiritual battles, the couple forgave the young man. God's grace ministered to the preacher as he poured out the Word of God to the men in the prison. Many were saved, including the young man who killed his daughter. After several years, the young man began to work with the couple and their prison ministry. Isn't being in ministry all about ministering God's grace even when wronged by others, and loving people you do not want to love?

An unforgiving heart shows no mercy. It wants to dictate God's grace. It is unyielding and stubborn. It won't let go of the past. When we are unwilling to forgive, we are refusing God's grace. God has forgiven us of all our sins and separated them from us as far as the east is from the west; and He no longer holds them against us. Our sins are eternally forgiven. God forgives and forgets. So, why are we not as gracious? Only by grace are we saved, only by grace are we not consumed by our enemies. The same grace of God that covers my life covers yours. God has called us to be a gracious people to live a life full of love, mercy, and peace. You that have unsettled unforgiving ways have not obeyed the commandment of Jesus. The Lord instructed us to forgive and keep on forgiving as many times as necessary to live in the liberty He paid for at Calvary. Let us learn to let go of all the grief and the bitterness and forgive them that hurt us, and let God do a mighty work in all that are involved.

The ministry of the Holy Spirit is to bring souls into a place of conviction and wholeness. To forgive is a choice. It is your choice to forgive and allow the Holy Spirit to minister healing to you. Without forgiveness, we would not have eternal life. God has forgiven us of a tremendous debt we could not pay. Jesus, by His own blood, paid our sin debt. The love of God transcends anything we can ever experience in our lifetime. When we look at the offenses against us, we will find that none can compare to the sin debt we owed to God. Jesus paid it all for us, and we owe all to Him!

Prayer:

Father, your Word says for me to fret not because of evildoers, neither be envious against the workers of inequity, for they will be judged by you. I ask, Father, that you forgive me for having an unforgiving heart. I release the bitterness I hold and ask for your help to love them that caused the pain and suffering I am experiencing. I choose to forgive, and I choose to forget everything in my past that has weighted my spirit. Just as you have forgiven me, I will forgive also. I move from this place of defeat into a new place of victory. I will bless those who curse me and love those who don't love me. I thank you, Father, that I am free to live in the liberty that you provided for me. Lord, I will live for you, and I seek to do your will. I am claiming that I will be full of love, compassion, mercy, and grace. I will be full of joy. Let me reach out and be a blessing in the lives of them that offended me. Let me fulfill the will you have for my life, in Jesus' name. Amen.

Daily encouragement /Further scripture study and readings:

Monday: Matthew 18:23–35
Tuesday: 2 Corinthians 2:5–8
Wednesday: Luke 6:35–38: Luke 23:33–34
Thursday: Ephesians 4:32
Friday: John 8:7, Hebrews 12:14
Saturday: Colossians 3:13
Sunday: 1 Corinthians 13:4–6

A True Disciple Won't Hate Me Because I'm Beautiful

"But he that hateth his brother is in darkness, and walketh in darkness, and knoweth not whither he goeth, because that darkness hath blinded his eyes." 1 John 2:11

Weight/Sin: **Hatred**
(Severe Dislike, Animosity, Discrimination, Abhor, Detest)

Inspiration:

Hatred has gone around the world and back again. It has caused many to perish and many communities to be destroyed. In world history, we remember the Holocaust, the most horrific hate crime committed, the goal to annihilate a whole nation of Jewish people. Then there were the genocides recorded in Africa of mass murders in remote places. Today in the news, we read of wars and rumors of wars in the Middle East all because of the hatred they have for the nation of Israel. Nations attacking other nations because they hate their nationality or their religious beliefs. We read extreme cults attacking people that live among them because they hate everyone that was born and believe differently than themselves.

In our country, in several states, it was reported national hate crimes were committed against churches full of innocent people. Police officers killing unarmed black men and women allegedly in self-defense, in the line of duty. Other places reported bombs that were planted and detonated in night clubs, theaters, governmental facilities; and other sightings told of shootings in different schools, restaurants, and other places all because of hate. God's Word is clear in telling us that all men are created equal, and all souls belong to God (Ezekiel 18:4). All can receive the full inheritance of heaven. God's Holy Word will teach us how to love and serve everyone no matter their ethnicity, color, gender, or nationality. All men are created equal and must be respected and treasured; that's God's way!

Hate is the opposite of God. He is love. How can you say that you love God if you're hating people? If you say you love God and hate your brother, then you are in darkness. 1 John 4:20–21 (ESV) reads, "If a man says I love God and hates his brother (or sister), he is a liar: for he that loves not his brother whom he has seen, how can he love God whom he has not seen? This commandment we have from him, that he who loves God loves his brother also." You cannot love God if you hate people. Jesus called for us to love even our enemies and pray for those that persecute us. In order to get our lives in line with the Word of God, we must know what it says. Only then are we able to put all things in our life into perspective. During the partaking of the last supper, Jesus said to the disciples: "A new commandment I give unto you, that you love one another; as I have loved you, that ye also love one another. By this shall all men know that you are my disciples, if you have love one to another" (John 13:34–35).

Love is the language of heaven. You will fulfill all the laws of God if you love thy neighbor as thyself. You will not sin against them but desire to help them in any way you can. Who is thy neighbor? Everyone you meet is your neighbor. God has given us an understanding that hate toward our fellowman/woman is an offense and a sin against Him. Hate has many spiritual repercussions (Matthew 5). Hatred will hold you and keep you in a place of unforgiveness. God has instructed us to forgive others as he has forgiven us our trespasses and sins (see the chapter on unforgiving). Hatred will stop your worship: Notice that in Matthew 5:24, you read that if you have an offense against anyone, the Word tells us to leave your gift at the altar, go and be reconciled with them, then return and make an offering of your gift. Jesus teaches us that having the right heart towards

God and other people is much more important in God's sight than your sacrifices and offerings to Him. Hatred hinders your prayers!

God teaches us to love our enemies. Pray for those that have used you and persecuted you. As you pray blessings on those who hurt you, you will find that hatred will not live in the presence of love. They will be blessed, and you will be blessed. Rejoice with others as they bless the Lord. Be encouraged to pray to the God of love and cast hate out of your life. Put the devil of hatred under your feet where he belongs! For God is not mocked. He is a God of love. Surrender your heart to God and sow seeds of love. You shall reap what you sow.

Prayer:

Father God, you are love. You have demonstrated the power of your love throughout the holy scriptures. Even in our sin, your love for us is unconditional. You love us with an everlasting love. I seek to be more like you. I ask for forgiveness of the hate I harbor in my heart. I empty my heart and forgive everyone who has personally violated me or my rights. I pray, let not my prayers be hindered. Show me how to bless those that have hurt me. I will obey your Word, and I will pray for them. Help me to heap coals of compassion on their heads. Because if they knew you, they too will put hate speedily away from them.

1 Peter 3:9 (NIV) reminds us "Do not repay evil with evil or insult with insult. On the contrary, repay evil with blessing, because to this you were called so that you may inherit a blessing." I will not render evil for evil. I pour blessings on my neighbors and acquaintances and you will reward me with blessings! Lord, I am full of remorse for harboring hateful feelings. I ask for a heart of compassion. I repent, and I lift my head toward the hills from whence cometh my help. My help is in the Lord. I thank you for saving me. Thank you for setting me free. I desire to worship you, God. I worship you in the beauty of your holiness! I have the spirit of truth inside me. Lord, I have love inside me, a Godly love that causes me to want to love everybody. What a mighty God you are that you will hear my prayer and answer

me (Jeremiah 33:3). I give you all the praise and all the glory because you are worthy, in Jesus' name. Amen.

Daily encouragement /Further scripture study and readings:

Monday: Leviticus 19:17
Tuesday: John 15:18
Wednesday Proverbs 26:24–26
Thursday: Romans 12:9–13
Friday: Matthew 5:44
Saturday: Ephesians 8:13
Sunday: 1 John 2:9

Go and Sin No More!

"If we confess our sins, He is faithful and just to forgive us our sins, and to cleanse us from all unrighteousness." 1 John 1:9

Weight/Sin: **Adultery**
(Extramarital Affair, Infidelity, Unfaithful, Liaison)

Inspiration:

Adultery is when a man or a woman willingly has sexual relations with anyone other than their spouse. There are no exceptions. Adultery is sin against God, sin against the spouse, and sin against the sanctity of matrimony. Adultery committed cannot be undone. The damage done can be seen throughout families of every nationality, creed, and walk of life. It has destroyed healthy homes, families, businesses, friendships, and relationships. The family unit was ordained by God Himself. He wants people to live a blessed life. God knows man's heart. Man seeks to satisfy the lusts of the flesh. God's will for man is to have self-control. Those who commit adultery or who are deeply hurt by their spouse's adultery often wonder about forgiveness, other consequences from the sin, or even divorce. When King David committed adultery, Nathan confronted David with the words of the Lord recorded in 2 Samuel 2:7–9, "You are the man! Thus, says the Lord God of Israel: I anointed you King over Israel, and I delivered you from the hand of Saul. I gave you your master's house and your master's wives into your keeping and gave you the house of Israel and Judah. And if that had been too little, I also would have given you much more." Look at all that God had done for David. He was convicted! David repented, and sinned no more.

A woman was caught in adultery, and her accusers were ready to stone her according to the Mosaic law. They took her to Jesus and told Him what she had done. Jesus replied to the accusers, "He without sin let him cast the first stone." They all slipped away, every one of them. Jesus then asked the woman, "Where are your accusers?" She replied, "There are none, Lord." Jesus said to her, "Neither do I condemn you, go and sin no more." (Read account in John 8:1–11). These words Jesus said to the woman who was caught in adultery, after the mob went away.

They are the same words He is speaking to us. Remove yourself from the adulterous affair. It is not God's will. God is waiting to forgive us and receive us back into the fold. Words of mercy are still written throughout the pages of the New Testament. God will not condemn us; He will welcome us with open arms. He will restore us back into the family of God and into our future. If we will just confess our sins, He is faithful and just to forgive us of our sins and to cleanse us from all unrighteousness!

Prayer:

Father, I repent of this evil I have done. Cleanse me from secret sins. I break off all relationships that are adulterous and immoral. Forgive me, Lord. My sins are as scarlet and as red as crimson, but I ask that you wash me, cleanse me that they be as wool and white as snow. I do not dismiss my wrongdoings, but I acknowledge my sin, accept the responsibility and the consequences for what I have done. I thank you for showing me my mistakes. Teach me in the way I should go. Surround me with songs of deliverance. I trust in you. Let your mercy and grace be a constant companion. Lord, you are good, and your mercy endures forever. Restore me to a place of trust and fidelity. Bring healing to those whom I have hurt with my past actions. "Have mercy on me, O God, according to your unfailing love; according to your great compassion blot out my transgressions" Psalm 51:1 (NIV). I pray in Jesus' name. Amen.

Daily encouragement / Further scripture study and readings:

Monday: 1 Corinthians 6:18, 7:1–40
Tuesday: 2 Samuel 12:1–9
Wednesday: Proverbs 6:24–29, 6:32
Thursday: Matthew 5:28, 19:9
Friday: Mark 10:1–12
Saturday: Hebrews 13:4
Sunday: Ephesians 5:5
(also, see lasciviousness, cheating, guilt, shame, fornication)

Lasciviousness, What Does It Mean?

"Walk in the Spirit, and ye shall not fulfill the lust of the flesh." Galatians 5:16

Weight/Sin: **Lasciviousness**
(Lewdness, Lustful, Indecent)

Inspiration:

The word *lascivious* is not in the newer translations of the Bible. However, it is mentioned seven times in the new testament of the King James Version Bible and referred to several more times by using related words. Immoral is one used the most, but lasciviousness is more than just immoral or indecent. It is far deeper than expressed wrongdoing. It is described as a person's behavior that is driven by thoughts of sex. The conduct of a man or woman, that is lustful and who display themselves in a lewd, indecent manner of a sexual nature. They have thoughts of lust, acting, and showing themselves to be lustful and cause others to lust. They are driven by licentious desires.

Lasciviousness was fervently condemned and had to be addressed by the early church. It had subtly crept into the congregation, causing the people to sin. Today, we see the same indecency. Lascivious behavior is seen among those in the pews, on the praise team, ushering our aisles, in youth ministries, and even in the pulpit. It is a serious sinful behavior, so serious that Jesus expressed disapproval of it in Mark 7:21–23. It is written, "For from within, out of the heart of men proceed evil thoughts, adulteries, fornications, murders, thefts, covetousness, wickedness, deceit, lasciviousness, an evil eye, blasphemy, pride, foolishness: All these evil things come from within, and defile the man."

The acts of the flesh will not inherit the kingdom of God (Galatians 5:19, 21). How intense and how one handles iniquity is all a matter of the heart. Jesus explains that the evil thoughts and intentions in the heart are what defiles the person. What is acted upon, starts first as a thought. There is a need for holy teaching on how we ought to conduct ourselves as becoming to a Christian. The Word says to come out from the world and be ye separated, for we are a peculiar people and a chosen generation (1 Corinthians 6:17; 2 Peter 2:9). We are instructed to "touch not, handle not, and taste not the unclean things of this world" (Colossians 2:21). Our loving Father has many children. Let us walk, pleasing to Him in all holiness. The saying goes, "Don't judge a book by its cover." Even though the genre and the cover give you an idea of what to expect inside the book, this metaphorical phrase means that you shouldn't prejudge the worth or value of something by its outward appearance alone.

People choose to dress in various fashions for numerous reasons. Misinterpretation can come based on what we see. Clothing generally expresses a person's values; clothing becomes a form of expression. As Christians, we are to represent God in all our actions: what we say, what we do, and how we dress. 1 Peter 3:1 (ESV) says, "Do not let your adorning be external…but let your adorning be the hidden person of the heart with the imperishable beauty of a gentle and quiet spirit, which in God's sight is very precious."

God can clean us up both inside and out. Matthew 23:26 says, "Blind Pharisee! First clean the inside of the cup and dish, and the outside also will be cleaned" (NIV). A person's appearance, either their physical attributes or how they are dressed, are not indicators of their inner being. We, as humans, are incredibly complex. While one can gaze upon us and make assumptions from our appearance, our spiritual (inner) man is not so apparent at first glance. We are known by the fruit of our actions! A tree is known by the fruit it bears. An apple tree produces apples, a pear tree, pears. Fig trees yield figs, and so on. We, too, are known by the fruit we bear. If we live by the flesh, walk in the flesh, we reap corruption. But if we live in the spirit and walk in the spirit of God, we shall reap life everlasting (Galatians 6:8).

Prayer:

Father, in the name of Jesus, I confess my sins before you. I desire to be pure and holy. That I may be an heir and a joint heir with Jesus Christ in the kingdom of God. I lift my voice to you and repent of all my sins. I ask that you cleanse me from lustful thoughts, lustful acts, and lustful deeds. May I never be the cause of someone falling into sin. Your Word clearly states that it is better for a millstone to be tied around one's neck, and they be cast into the sea, than to be found to offend any of your little ones, causing them to sin. In you, Lord, I shall live a good and decent life. And even now, I pray for myself and others who may be living in lasciviousness. You can set me free, and I know if we come to you, we will be made free. Let my life be a witness of what the power of God can do. If you did it for others, God, I know you'll do it for me. Amen.

Daily encouragement / Further scripture study and readings:

Monday: Mark 7:21–23
Tuesday: 1 Thessalonians 4:4
Wednesday: 2 Corinthians 12:20–21
Thursday: Galatians 5:19–21
Friday: Ephesians 4:19–24
Saturday: 1 Peter 4:3–6
Sunday: Jude 1:4–5

Don't Defile the Temple

"Know ye not, that your body is the temple of the Holy Ghost?" 1 Corinthians 6:19a

Weight/Sin: **Fornication**
(Whoredom, Harlotry, Illicit Sex)

Inspiration:

It is almost impossible these days to watch a primetime show on television and not see the main character in suggestive, compromising positions, and eventually in a sexual scene. The most popular secular music today sings about sexuality. Sexual images are all around, from our electronic devices, commercials, reality television, print materials, movies, billboards, seemingly everywhere.

Years ago, in an evangelistic crusade, I recall the preacher saying that we are living in a sex-saturated society. I have noticed even the people in the church, when confronted with their lifestyle of fornication, often reply, "I have needs. My body has urges," suggesting that it is something they do not want to give up. There seems to be no shame or embarrassment in flaunting one's true feelings on illicit sex. It displeases God when we live in the passions of our flesh and carry out the desires of the body and mind. Fornication is a sin against your own body. We have pleased our carnal man so often that the flesh is demanding to be satisfied. It is a fleshly appetite that is out of control.

Paul wrote in Galatians 5:24 that "those who are in Christ should crucify the flesh with all its affections and its lusts, bringing it into subjection under the Holy Ghost." "Know ye not that you are the temple of the Holy Ghost, which is in you, which ye have of God, and ye are not your own?" Know that your bodies are members of Christ? Shall you take the members of Christ and make them members of a harlot? Flee fornication! You are not your own. You have been bought with a price, therefore glorify God in your body and in your spirit, which is God's" (1 Corinthians 6:15–20). When we accepted Christ, the Holy Spirit came to dwell inside of us. We house the Holy Spirit. We serve a holy God that demands us to be holy as He is holy, separated from all sin. His spirit will not dwell in an unclean temple! "We are redeemed, bought back from the enemy of our souls" (Psalms 107:2).

Yes! We have been purchased by the blood of Jesus Christ to live free from sin. Redeemed, purchased by the blood of the Lamb. Crucify the flesh and take your life back. Bring your body and all its urges under the subjection of the Spirit of God. God, being rich in mercy because of His love for us, stands ready to make us alive together with Christ again. Be determined to walk as Jesus walked, free from sin. We are the redeemed of the Lord, hallelujah! Let the redeemed of the Lord say so!

Prayer:

Father, I am a member in the body of Christ. I have trusted in my flesh and yielded my members to sin against my body and against your Word. I ask for complete forgiveness. Forgive me for quenching the Holy Spirit, for convicting me of my sins. I repent for all I have done and all the deception I may have caused by lying to satisfy my fleshly desires causing others to commit fornication. May this be the true desire of my heart, to be holy as you are holy. I am thankful that you have given me the newness of life. I am redeemed. I am in the body of Christ. I will conduct myself as I ought according to the Word of God. Help me to live a sanctified life that is acceptable in your sight. I give you my heart, Lord. Heal my soul that I may gain the strength to go on. I shall be mindful of the things of God because I know you are mindful of me. I shall crucify my flesh daily. It shall no more have rule over me. Hallelujah! I am redeemed, in Jesus' name. Amen.

Daily encouragement/Further scripture study and readings:

Monday: Romans 1:29–32
Tuesday: 1 Corinthians 5:1–2, 6:13
Wednesday: Galatians 5:19
Thursday: Ephesians 5:3
Friday: Colossians 3:5–6
Saturday: 1 Thessalonians 4:3
Sunday: Jude 1:7
(also, see lasciviousness, infidelity, cheating, shame)

When You Just Can't Seem to Get Over It!

"I have great heaviness and continued sorrow in my heart." Romans 9:2

Weight/Sin: **Grief**
(Intense Sorrow, Bereavement, Misery, Vexation)

Inspiration:

A mosquito, a bee, or a wasp can land on the skin, sting, and be gone before human reflexes kick in to swat it away. As quick and as fast a sting sometimes, so it is with a sudden tragedy. Grief can overtake us suddenly and leave us emotionally stunned and peering through a fog of sentiments. Many times, tragedy comes so unexpectedly. The suddenness of a death can leave loved ones in a daze, and they are so distraught that they may question God. Why has a child been taken? Why does a young man or a good husband pass away? Why do so many die young? Why do people have to suffer with terminal illnesses? Why did "this" have to happen?

We usually associate grief with death, but there are so many other reasons one may suffer with a loss. Such as the ending of a marriage, destruction of a home, a prodigal child, financial ruin, or a devastating illness. No matter how calamity approaches comes the destruction, bereaving the pain, the mourning of intense sorrow, and the struggle resulting from it all are real. There is no better example of grief than what is found in the book of Job. He is the chief of grief and yet the patriarch of patience (James 5:11). He experienced the sting of sudden and intense sorrow. He had it all, by the world's interpretation of success, and lost it all in one day. A tornado took down his houses and killed his ten children. Robbers stole his cattle, his camels and killed his servants. Lightning destroyed his livestock and the attending shepherds. His body was afflicted with boil sores from the crown of his head to the very soles of his feet. Then three friends that came to comfort him became his accusers. Through all his grief and sufferings, the Word tells us that Job sinned not against God. He did not blame God but simply said, "The Lord giveth and the Lord hath taken away; Blessed be the name of the Lord" (Job 1:21).

Yes, he wondered why. Yes, he suffered greatly, but he held onto his integrity and his trust in the Almighty. Blessed be the name of the Lord! Saint of God, you have permission to grieve your losses and cry out your pain. The struggle is real when you cannot get over a loss. For we know that grief comes, but it does not have to leave scars. God never intended for it to damage a person. It was never expected that man should live in a constant state of grief. Pain is not always a punishment. God allowed the people of Israel to mourn forty days for their leaders: Aaron, Moses, the patriarchs, the prophets, and kings. But they also experienced pain because of their bad choices.

It is healthy and normal to mourn a loss. It is not a weakness to express emotional, physical, or even spiritual sorrow. Do not give up on God because he won't give up on you! It is a good thing to admit and confess your true feelings to God, to others, and to yourself. Don't harness your misery and allow Satan to hold you captive in your grief. Just as temporary as the grave to a saint, so is mourning. We still have hope to see a better tomorrow.

Prayer:

Father, how gracious you are. It has been so hard to move on. The grief has been so great. I don't know which way to turn sometimes or how to go on living. I feel lost inside. I admit, I struggle, and don't know if I can let it go. In myself, I can't get past the pain, but in you, I can. With the help of the Holy Spirit, I'm coming boldly to your throne of grace in my hour of need. In Christ Jesus, I know there is healing for me. I ask for my every wound to be healed. I pray for strength to overcome and peace to comfort my soul.

Lord, I release this grief to you right now that I may receive joy and gladness. I take off the garment of heaviness and put on my garment of praise. I trade my mourning for gladness and seek rest and peace of mind. Lord, your grace is sufficient for me, for your power is made perfect in my weakness. Lord, let your power rest on me, for when I am weak, then I am strong in you! I declare that the struggle is over! The battle is won, and I have the victory in Jesus' name. Amen.

Daily encouragement /Further scripture study and readings:

Monday: Psalm 126:5–6
Tuesday: Ecclesiastes 3:1–4
Wednesday: Isaiah 53:3, 61:1–3
Thursday: Psalm 34:18
Friday: Matthew 5:4
Saturday: 2 Corinthians 1:3–4
Sunday: Revelation 21:4

Behind the Smile Lies a Clever but Cruel Tongue

"Let no corrupting talk come out of your mouths, but only such as is good for building up, as fits the occasion, that it may give grace to those who hear." Ephesians 4:29 (ESV)

Weight/Sin: **Condescending**
(Belittle, Patronizing, Pretentious, Denigrating)

Inspiration:

"Don't take everybody to be your friend" was advice my mother spoke to her children often as we were growing up. Mothers can somehow see through the mask of the friends their children bring home. A word to the wise was always sufficient for us. There are people, in the company of others, that will smile in your face and cunningly humiliate you just for the upstaging of themselves. Behind their smile is a clever but cruel tongue. They seem to have a knack and the wittiest ways to put you down with a patronizing remark. It is a truly degrading experience.

We are disciples of Christ. We are duly informed in the Bible how we ought to behave ourselves. John tells us to love one another (2 John 5); Paul tells us to encourage one another and build one another up (Thessalonians 5:11). He also tells us to instruct one another, since we want to see everyone mature in Christ (Colossians 1:28). We should stir one another up to love and good works (Hebrews 10:24). So much damage is done to others with an unruly, evil tongue. Stop!

In the name of love and for the love of God! No Christian should verbally attack others. Stop your condescending actions. Halt the humiliation and pretentious ways. We are called to heal and not to afflict. We are to encourage and not discourage, to help build up and not to tear down. The voice and tongue are gifts from God and instruments to praise Him. Let us edify and speak peace and blessings into each other's lives. Let's use our tongues to glorify God. The power of life and death lies in the tongue!

Follow Christ by doing spiritual good for someone, by initiating, teaching, correcting, modeling, loving, humbling ourselves, counseling, and influencing, and in doing so, there is no room for condescending, patronizing, or denigrating others!

Prayer:

Father, in the name of Jesus, I ask for your forgiveness for every time I have used my words to speak unkindness to another. There is never an excuse to do this when you have already shared in your Word, "But the tongue can no man tame. It is an unruly evil, full of deadly poison." Because I have shown that my tongue is difficult to control and realize that I need deliverance from this weight of denigrating and being patronizing to others, I cry out to you, my only source of strength and deliverance. Help me, oh Lord, I ask for wisdom in my exchanges with others, to speak soft and kind words, to build up and never tear down. I want to always demonstrate your unfailing and unconditional love through me in all of my ways. Amen.

Daily encouragement/Further scripture study and readings:

Monday: Proverbs 11:12
Tuesday: Romans 14:10
Wednesday: Psalm 22:24
Thursday: James 4:11–12
Friday: 1 Timothy 4:12–14
Saturday: Titus 3:1–15
Sunday: 1 Peter 2:1–25

Dominate Your Own Destiny

"Behold all souls are mine; as the soul of the father, so also the soul of the son is mine."
Ezekiel 18:4a

Weight/Sin: **Possessive**
(Overbearingly Protective, Usurping, Dominating, Control)

Inspiration:

We are living in a society that advertises the newest, the biggest, and latest gadgets. The newest fashions, cars, and other material things because we are a materialistic society. The more we see, the more the appetite for things thrives. We want it, so we buy. We have become over consumers. We do not want to be without. We get what we want when we want it, and we have become possessive with what belongs to us, and for some, this behavior has carried over into their relationships with the people in their lives. Possessiveness is what it's called, and men are not the only ones that have shown to be possessive in relationships. Women can be possessive as well.

Some people live under a possessive hand. This is beyond jealousy. When a man or woman live under this rule, they are monitored in everything they do, including everywhere they go. They have no freedom. They are prisoners in their own homes. People are not items of property for others to make claims or demands! "Know that the Lord Himself is God. It is He who made us and not we ourselves; we are His people and the sheep of His pasture" (Psalm 100:3, NASV). Even the evils of slavery were broken by the teachings of the gospel through the missions of Christianity. Paul wrote to Philemon how the working of God converted a runaway slave, Onesimus (see the book of Philemon). He implored Philemon to receive him back as a Christian brother. Yes, he was still a slave or servant, but he was treated with respect and without the heavy yoke of bondage.

That dominating, controlling, and manipulative spirit of possessiveness is a curse to all who endure it. "If any man shall come after me let him deny himself, pick up his cross, and follow after me" (Matthew 16:24). The words of Jesus instruct us to deny ourselves and honor and respect others. What does it profit or benefit a man if he gains the whole world and loses his own soul? God gave us all things in this life to love and to enjoy. If you are blessed with a spouse, children, and all the frills of life, be a blessing and not a hard task master with possessive ownership. Let Jesus reign in your home, bringing in freedom. It is for us to build a home with prayer, being the watchmen over our households by directing and guiding our families by the Holy Spirit and all that God entrusted into our hands.

All things belong to God anyway, "All souls are mine" (Ezekiel 18:4). All things were created by Him and for Him (Colossians 1:16). We were all created to be free in Christ Jesus. We were created to be God's property for His glory. God is in control of all things in heaven and on earth (Psalm 115:3). When you understand that you have but one life to give to the Lord, wouldn't you want it to be well pleasing to Him? We cannot be possessive over the relationships in our lives, but we can take responsibility and dominate our own affairs. There is a destiny in Him that has already been planned out for each of us (Jeremiah 29:11). It is time to lay aside every weight and sin that so easily beset us. Spend precious time with loved ones demonstrating love in all that we do, for the time is growing nigh for the Lord Jesus to return. Be the captain of your own ship. Guide and instruct your crew and dominate your own destiny!

Prayer:

Heavenly Father, in Psalm 24:1, you tell us that, you are Lord overall. "The earth is the Lord's and the fullness thereof and that they that dwell therein." Everything belongs to you. I have shown to be possessive over people and things. I understand now that truly all things belong to you, and you have made me the caretaker of the things I have. I have snatched responsibilities out of the hands of my spouse and dominated over all we possess. I have usurped authority in an unhealthy manner in relationships. I confess that I have a dominating and jealous attitude. I know that jealousy can cause ruin in relationships. I thank you that you are a loving and patient Father. You still love me in spite of myself. I thank you that you created us to be free. You have given us the Word of God and wisdom to govern our lives and train our children accordingly.

I am yours, Lord. Everything I am and all that you have blessed me with. Lord, I pray for forgiveness to live the way you created me to live, and all those that are under my care to do the same. Teach me to raise my children according to your Word, and to be a nurturer of my family. Help me to guide them and godly instruct them that they may seek you, to find their destinies in you. And that I may find my destiny in you in rearing godly children who won't continue in this ungodly character trait that they may have witnessed. Lord, deliver me from this weight that I might run uninhibited for the prize of the high calling, which is in Christ Jesus! Amen.

Daily encouragement/Further scripture study and readings:

Monday: Acts 26:20
Tuesday: Romans 12:10, 8:1–39
Wednesday: Titus 1:16
Thursday: Ephesians 1:11
Friday: James 4:6
Saturday: 1 Timothy 3:1–10
Sunday: 2 Corinthians 4:4
(also, see jealousy, possessive, bossiness)

Eye for an Eye, Tooth for a Tooth? No, Lord, You Fight My Battles!

"Dearly beloved, avenge not yourselves, but rather give place unto wrath: for it is written, vengeance is mine; I will repay, saith the Lord."
Romans 12:19

Weight/Sin: **Vengeful**
(Vindictive, Spiteful, Antagonistic, Maliciousness)

Inspiration:

Have you ever, in all your days, seen so many people who want to live by the code of the old, old west? The history stories tell of the Wild West and the gold rush days, how some men were wild and ruthless. Motion picture promoters picked up on the plots, and western shows of the twentieth century became popular. It made for great family entertainment in radio listening, theater, and television viewing. The wandering straight shooters, gunslingers, sharp shooters, hired guns all with the big black hats. These bad guys who despised the law, lived under a law of revenge. The vindicator would wander into town seeking revenge: "An eye for and eye, a tooth for a tooth!" is the law they lived by. They did not seek out justice but sought to get even. This was the usual plots written for the old western shows and movies. In the old west, the vengeful never won.

Again, I ask, have you ever seen so many people who harbor vengeance in their hearts as they do today? The streets are not as wild as the old west, officially credited by the laws of our land. People are not willing to forgive (see the weight on unforgiving). They seem to have no regard for their fellow man. Vengeful hearts are found in the church. Even Christians are seen holding grudges, battling one another, and having attitudes with intentions to say or retaliate with evil. This is not living according to the code of the kingdom of God. Jesus taught if someone slaps your face, turn the other cheek. If someone took your coat, offer them your cloak also (Matthew 5:39). When we are done wrong, then it is up to us to forgive. It is an opportunity for God to be glorified through our lives. When bad things happen in our lives and situations seem hopeless, we may be tempted to doubt God. But Christians must remember that no problem is too great for God!

In Exodus 14:14, Moses tells the children of Israel, "The Lord will fight for you; you need only to be still." At that moment, the Red Sea was before them, and the Egyptian army behind them. The Israelites were in what seemed to be an impossible situation; one that appeared hopeless and inescapable. When we trust God to fight our battles, it becomes life-altering for us when God provides a way for our escape, our confidence, and our faith soars in Him! Avoid the pit falls and snares of the devil. A vengeful heart never wins! Do not take vengeance upon yourselves but leave it to the hands of God. "Vengeance is mine," says the Lord, "I will repay" (Romans 12:19). Even James wrote "count it all joy when you fall into divers temptations; knowing that the trying of your faith works patience" (James 1:2–3). This is how we win over the enemy. Let God reign in our life no matter what the devil brings into our paths. Patience is a virtue. Galatians 6:9 says, "And let us not be weary in well doing." Be patient in well doing even in sufferings, be counted with the righteous, and "in due season, you shall reap" a harvest that's everlasting, if you faint not.

Prayer:

Father, in the name of Jesus, I feel I have been done an injustice. I have been wronged. And I have harbored a vindictive spirit. I humbly approach your throne and ask for forgiveness and mercy in this hour. Help me not to seek revenge. I release now the vengeance I harbor in my heart. Teach me your ways and to show your love to all that have wronged me, and I them. I refuse to fall into the snare of the devil and continue to take matters into my own hands. I acknowledge your Word that declares vengeance is mine, says the Lord, I will repay. For all the times I reacted in vengeance, forgive my trespasses and sins and help me to forgive them that trespassed against me. Lord, help me to see people through the eyes of love. I desire to be a blessing and not to cause hurt nor pain. Cleanse me of all my unrighteousness that I can have a pure heart and clean hands before you. Lord, I thank you for your grace as I surrender. Fill me with your Holy Spirit that I may have the strength to endure every temptation and be an overcomer in this life. In Jesus' name I pray. Amen.

Daily encouragement/Further scripture study and readings:

Monday: Deuteronomy 32:35
Tuesday: Romans 12:19–21
Wednesday: Matthew 5:39–44
Thursday: Hebrews 6:1, 10:30–31
Friday: 1 Peter 2:22–23
Saturday: James 1:2–6
Sunday: Revelations 18:4

If You Are the Judge, Where Is Your Robe?

"Do not judge others, and you will not be judged"
Matthew 7:1 (NLT)

Weight/Sin: **Judgmental**
(Critical, Fault-Finding, Overly-Critical)

Inspiration:

We live because of the grace of God and because God freely grants us grace daily. It is not of our own accord that we even live! Therefore, if we cannot take care of our own selves, how can we stand in judgement of others? Judging and even condemning others who are in a struggle with sin or iniquity are not to be found among believers. What judging does is counteract the grace of God given so freely to each of us. As God so freely gives grace to us and extends His mercy, we are to do the same to others. It can be very confusing when we hear that as Christians we are not to "judge" others, but we are to discern and judge what is truth.

The Word of God tells us to confront other's sin with truth and love. Jesus reminds us to look at our own sin before standing in judgement of others. Remember the Golden Rule? Most learned in our early years of Sunday School, "Do unto others as you would have them do unto you" (Luke 6:31). We should have learned that early in life, but what happened that we are now critical of others? Do not condemn, judge, or hate others. If you are led by God to correct someone, execute the correction in love. God loves us, and the scripture reminds us that "there is therefore now no condemnation to them which are in Christ Jesus, who walk not after the flesh, but after the Spirit" (Romans 8:1). Although we all have sinned and fallen short of the glory of God, we must not judge others because we ourselves have shortcomings. Don't allow your witness to be hindered by having a condemning tongue. Our words should reflect Christ and direct others to Him, and not away from Him. At one time or another, all of us may have been a victim of a "critical tongue". Remember how that made you feel? Don't judge others, and you will not be judged!

Prayer:

I thank you, Father, for your never-ending grace extended to all of us. I thank you for loving me enough not to judge me of my sinful deeds and giving freely to me your loving grace! Help me to put away all sinful acts of judging and condemnation of others. You tell us to judge not, lest we be judged. This sinful self-righteous act of judging others I lay it aside now, and with your help and your wisdom, I will not fall again. Lord, help me to perfect my witness to others that it won't be hindered by my shortcomings. May I never forget how you rescued me from sin and shame as I came to know of your wonderful grace. May I always find words to introduce others to your wonderful love for them. I want to declare your grace boldly to all that will hear, in Jesus' name. Amen.

Daily encouragement /Further scripture study and readings:

Monday: Matthew 7:1–5
Tuesday: John 8:1–8
Wednesday: Luke 6:31–36
Thursday: Romans 2:1–3, Romans 14:1–13
Friday: Proverbs 31:9
Saturday: Galatians 6:1–6
Sunday: James 4:11–12

You Can't Smell the Smoke on My Clothes

"If you are insulted because of the name of Christ, you are blessed, for the Spirit of glory and of God rests on you." 1 Peter 4:14, (NIV)

Weight/Sin: **Dejection**
(Despondence, Discouraged, Depressed, Low In Spirit)

Inspiration:

We can choose to feel despondent when we are insulted by someone because of our belief in Christ, or we can choose to see what a blessing it is for someone to identify you so closely with Christ that they treat you like they treated Him. What joy to be so closely associated with Christ! We are to take on the character of Christ in our times of persecution. Take an example from the Bible of the three Hebrew boys, Shadrach, Meshach, and Abednego. They were cast into a fiery furnace heated seven times hotter by decree of the evil King Nebuchadnezzar because they refused to worship his idol god. They took a stand for their belief in God. They knew their fate, but they trusted God. They knew that God was able to deliver them.

God uses our suffering to refine us and to make us more like Him. Our fiery trials are not in vain. Speaking of fire, it can be a consuming force! When a natural fire is out of control, it is known to destroy, annihilate, and wipe off the face of the earth anything in its path. It leaves complete ruin. Sometimes one can feel dejected, discouraged, and low in spirit. This feeling can come upon you after any type of rejection such as a love interest, desired job, or anything that you set your heart to receive and it doesn't come out as you expect. You may feel that you have been through the fire and the flames of life. This spirit of dejection has "engulfed" you, leaving you feeling discouraged, grievous, and unworthy.

Fire tends to draw curiosity out of people. People will gather amid your troubles to assess the damage (read about Job in the Bible). They gather to see how "singed" you are, to see if they can detect the smell of smoke in your clothes! It may seem like nothing is going your way. Once during our teenage years, my brother was sitting on the couch sulking. My very wise father saw him and inquired, "What's the matter, son?" My brother answered, "Nothing is going my way!" My father said to my brother, "Well, son, if nothing is going your way, you may need to turn and go another way." Often in life, we may need to assess our direction to make sure we are on the *right path*. Make sure we are seeking God for His divine direction for us, or we can easily begin to feel discouraged. Proverbs 3:5–6 says, "Trust in the Lord with all of your heart and lean not to your own understanding but in all thy ways acknowledge Him and He shall direct thy path".

You will emerge victoriously from the weight of rejection because you are walking in the will of God for your life. If we want to come out of the "fiery" trials of life without smelling of smoke, then we must invite Jesus into the fire with us. God will take the heat out of the fire and the smell out of the smoke! As a former teacher, I would teach fire safety to children. One catch phrase was used to help them to remember what to do in case of a fire: "Get down low, and go, go, go!" This phrase is applicable to the fires of life too! If you find yourself in a "fiery" situation in your life, get down on your knees and go to the Lord in prayer! Purpose in your heart that you fear not what man can do to you, speak about you, or even how they act toward you, know that God is on your side!

You may feel that you have been through the fire and the flames of life, feel dejected, powerless, and unworthy. But when you are walking in the will of God for your life, you will emerge victoriously from the weight of rejection! Hold your head up, you have come out of the fire. You have not even been "singed!" When God is on your side, the fire can't touch you! Walk today in the victory wherein the Lord has made you free!

Prayer:

Father, in the name of Jesus, I stand against feelings of dejection, despondency, discouragement, and lowliness of spirit that comes to mind in judgment of me. Lord, I repent before you for any offense that I may have done in transgression of your law. With all my heart, I diligently seek to do your will. I confess my worth, because I am a child of the King! I am a child of the Most High God who executes judgment from your throne! Lord, I don't understand this dejection, but I know your goodness extended to me.

Help me to replace these feelings with your truth of your undeniable love for me, and as I stand still, you will fight for me! "Plead my cause, O Lord, with them that strive with me: fight against them that fight against me. For without cause have they hid for me their net in a pit, which without cause they have digged for my soul. But in mine adversity, they rejoiced, and gathered themselves together against me, and I knew it not; they did tear me, and ceased not" (Psalm 35:1, 7, 15). Lord, I seek your deliverance from my adversary! Thank you for sending your Word to heal and to deliver us from all of our troubles (Psalm 107:20). We take comfort in knowing that you are a righteous judge who will avenge all evil. We must forgive others and stand steadfast in your assurance of deliverance. I believe the plans that you have for me are plans of good and not evil. God, I thank you for your guidance as I conduct business in my public and private life. I will always acknowledge you as I contemplate my path in life. I seek your will and direction.

God, turn this situation away from me and give me favor among people. Your favor is like a shield that protects us from the wiles of the enemy; whose maneuvers and tactics cannot penetrate or hinder the plans that you have for me. I claim my wholeness and speak to my brokenness, and the spirit of dejection must flee from me! I stand against feelings of inadequacy, failure, defeat, and mediocrity.

I confess my worth because I am your child, a child of the King! I am a child of the Almighty God who executes judgement from your throne! Lord, according to your Word, you will cause my enemies who rise up against me to be defeated before my face. They shall come out against me one way and flee before me seven ways! Lord, thank you for being faithful in keeping your covenant and extending your mercies unto all that love you and keep your commandments to a thousand generations, according to your Word, in Jesus' mighty name! Amen.

Daily encouragement /Further scripture study and readings:

Monday: Proverbs 3:5–6
Tuesday: Jeremiah 29:11
Wednesday: Daniel 3:26–27
Thursday: Psalm 35:1–28
Friday: 2 Corinthians 15:11–15
Saturday: 2 Peter 2:10
Sunday: Ephesians 2:10

"Fear and Dread, Get Out of My Head"

"For God hath not given us a spirit of fear, but of power, and of love and of a sound mind." 2 Timothy 1:7

Weight/Sin: **Fear**
(Dread, Terror, Trepidation, Horror, Distress)

    I think everyone has experienced fear at some time in their lives. It can be perceived or a very real danger, nevertheless I believe it all starts in your mind.

    Fear can be debilitating if we "build" it up in our thoughts, fear turns into dread and dread is like fear on steroids! The scripture reminds us in 2 Timothy 1:7 that, "For God hath not given us a spirit of fear, but of power and of love and of a sound mind." A sound mind will cause us to think rationally and began to reason, in order to protect ourselves from allowing fear to turn into dread! My husband once shared a story with me, when he was a young boy, he and his brother were returning home from a friend's house. Dusk started to settle in as the clouds from day began to cover the sun's light. As they scurried down the dark road, he spotted something flickering and flapping against the branches on the side of the road! The sounds "seemed" amplified and he *thought* "something is fighting to get to us" as their hearts were racing, he grabbed his brother's hand and ran as fast as they could towards home!

    The next morning as they walked to school down the same road, that "scary, flickering, flapping" thing was only a plastic bag caught in the thicket! Oh, how our thoughts can run away with us when we are facing the unknown! The enemy will cause fear to overtake us and consume our thoughts, by creating a falsehood that appears real.

God is our only defense against fear as He gives us the power to overcome fear. God will comfort us in the times of our anxiety and will provide a way for our escape from the thoughts that paralyze our thinking. The sound mind that He gives us will allow us to think clearly and to remember His promises in Joshua 1:9, "Have I not commanded thee? Be strong and courageous. Do not be frightened, and do not be dismayed, for the LORD your God is with you wherever you go."

As God led the children of Israel out of Egypt into their promised land, they encountered many fears. In our Christian life we too, are led out of sin so that we might enjoy a life more abundant. It was never God's plan that we remain in the wilderness of our spiritual experience. God's promise to every Christian, "I come that they may have life, and it more abundantly" (John 10:10b ESV). We can be assured of God's protection when we put our trust in Him. Some Christians never receive the fullness of God's plan for them, because they are walking in fear, not faith. In the Christian's life we walk in the promises of God's provisions of victory and deliverance! Rest and victory can be enjoyed in the life of every believer as we enjoy the promises and presence of the Lord in our lives. Don't allow fear to abide, fear and dread, get out of my head! I am a child of the King!

Prayer:

Father in the name of Jesus, what an awesome God you are that you made us in your image and in your likeness. You are God and God alone, there is none above you! I reject this spirit of fear that comes to my mind. I remind myself that you have not given me a spirit of fear but of power and of love and of a sound mind!

Lord I do not want to be perceived as one who has no faith. I stand on the promises in Psalm 91:4–6 that you will cover me with your feathers and under your wings shall I trust. Your truth is my shield and buckler. I will not be afraid for the terror by night nor the arrow that flieth by day; nor the pestilence that walked in darkness, nor the destruction that wasteth at noonday. I thank you Lord that you are holding me in your righteous right hand! Lord you said in Isaiah 14:3 that you will give me rest from fear and bondage in my life. Lord you are my confidence, my assurance in you I will trust and you shall keep my foot from slipping! Amen.

Daily encouragement / Further scripture study and readings:

Monday: Deuteronomy 31:6
Tuesday: Hebrews 13:6
Wednesday: John 14:27
Thursday: I Peter 5:7
Friday: Psalm 94:19
Saturday: Psalm 56:3
Sunday: Leviticus 26:6

An Invitation to Discipleship

Do you know Jesus?

Have you received Jesus Christ into your heart? Have you heard that He was made sin for you that in Him you might be made the righteous of God? (2 Corinthians 5:21). If not, please accept this invitation to receive Him as Lord and Savior of your life today! Simply confess this prayer for salvation and by faith you are saved.

A Prayer for Salvation

Heavenly Father, I come to you in the name of your Son, Jesus. Your Word says, "Whosoever shall call on the name of Jesus shall be saved" (Acts 2:21). I am calling out to you, Lord, today! According to Romans 10:9–10., "If thou shalt confess with thy mouth the Lord Jesus, and shalt believe in thy heart that God raised Him from the dead, thou shalt be saved." I confess right now that Jesus is Lord in my heart, and that God raised Him from the dead. I pray and ask that you come into my heart and be Lord over my life! I am now reborn! I am now a believer in Christ Jesus! I am a child of the Almighty God! I am now a Christian, saved by God's loving grace, in Jesus' name. Amen.

You will never be the same again! Now go and tell someone what you have done. If you are not an active member of a church, find a good Bible-teaching, faith-believing, Spirit-filled church in which you can grow. Become a faithful part of a church family who will love and care for you as you learn, love, and care for the things of God. It is God's perfect plan for your life!

Prayer Changes Things!

Prayer is God's proposal to man to bring about change that His will be done in the earth. We are told to pray without ceasing, praying with all manner of prayers and supplications, making our requests known to God. When we engage in prayers, supplications, and intercessions, we should pray according to the Word, in faith, believing that we have the promise that God hears us. We may not know how and when the answers will come, but the assurance is that God will answer in His timing and according to His will.

1 Timothy 2:1–2 tells us to first pray for all those in authority over us that we may live a peaceable life, and they may draw from the Word of God the wisdom to make righteous decisions needed to govern the people of our land. Start by praying for all those in leadership positions, from the president to the police officers that patrol our streets. Pray that they'll be surrounded by godly advisors, and they'll come to know Jesus in the pardon of their sins. Begin to pray daily. The Bible says, "Men ought to always pray and not faint!" To keep from fainting or surrendering your now "saved" life into the clutches of Satan, begin a daily prayer time. If you find it hard to garner the "right" words to say, just speak from your heart, God hears you! If the words come slow and even few, you can pray the scriptures to gain strength in your new walk with the Lord. Whenever you pray, asking God for anything, find a scripture correlation to your request and learn to pray the scriptures. Use the power of God's word to combat the enemy. We will commit to letting go of everything that is not like God. So that we can run this race to the finish. Prayer changes things, so lay aside every weight and sin that may hinder our prayer life. **"Let It All Go!" What are you "weighting" for?**

A Daily Prayer of Confession

O Lord my God, how excellent is your name in all the earth! Who hath set thy glory above the heavens (Psalm 8:1). You are our redeemer, ready with open arms to receive us again to you. We come to you in an act of obedience, as you invite us to come boldly to your throne of grace that we might obtain mercy and find grace in our time of need (Hebrews 4:16). We seek your forgiveness as we have all sinned and fallen short of your glory (Romans 3:23). God, I confess my weights and sins to you, knowing that you will readily forgive me (Psalm 32:5). Lord, just as you forgive me, I forgive others (Matthew 6:12) and confess my sin before you so my prayers are not hindered (James 5:16).

"Withhold not thou tender mercies from me, O Lord: let thy loving kindness and thy truth continually preserve me. Be pleased, O Lord, to deliver me: O Lord make haste to help me. Let them be ashamed and confounded together that seek after my soul to destroy it, let them be driven backward and put to shame that wish me evil." (Psalm 40:11, 13–14). Lord change our hearts and minds to love others as you have loved us; for when we genuinely love others, it covers a multitude of faults (1Peter 4:8) and demonstrates our being perfected in you. Lord, help us to be strong and courageous and not afraid, for you have not abandoned us, you will never leave nor forsake us (Joshua 1:9). Help us, dear Lord, to grow more into your likeness and grant us the courage and power that we need to do your will. We have all sinned and deserve your judgement, but you, being gracious, sent your Son to pay our sin debt; not just mine but to all who believe and trust in you (1 John 2:2).

Prayer reminds us that without your spirit working in our lives, we will fail! We were once stained by the consequences of sin, but now we confess to being washed by the blood of the Lamb of God because of His great love for us (Revelation 1:5). Lord, your love for us keeps us grounded in the beauty of holiness and keeps us in a humble receptive posture before you. Help us to look beyond ourselves, considering others just as Jesus, our example, relinquished His will to do the will of the Father (Luke 22:42).

Lord, we bring to you our brokenness and our inability to save ourselves. We confess our trust in you with all our hearts, as we lay aside our carnal confidence, to acknowledge you in all that we do, knowing that you will direct our paths (Proverbs 3:5–6). Lord, grant to us the confidence to know that we possess the power from you to lay aside every weight and sin and the faith to believe that our broken lives are made whole in you. Lord, you made us to have dominion over the works of your hands and have put all things under our feet. (Psalm 8:6). Lord, we will wait on you for renewed strength that will cause us to mount up with wings as eagles; as we run and not be weary; and as we walk and not faint (Isaiah 40:31). We cancel all satanic assignments that the enemy has planned. All his plans designed to keep us "weighted down", are thwarted, in Jesus' name. We command all satanic attacks on our families, finances, health, communities, and our futures, to cease and desist. God, you sent your Word to heal us from all of Satan's destructions (Psalm 107:20). We stand firmly on your promises. We are overcomers from every attack. We are victorious over the adversary. If we stand still, you will fight for us (Exodus 14:14). We are more than conquerors through Him that loved us (Romans 8:37)!

According to Romans 8:28, we know that even in our trials and sufferings, all things will work together for the good because we love you and are called according to your purposes. So, we will approach our darkest valley moments with confidence knowing that nothing can happen to us that is not permitted by you, our loving Father, for our good. Therefore, we live in anticipation of your goodness, as you "will hasten your word to perform it" (Jeremiah 1:12). In Jesus' name. Amen.

Conclusion

Some weights and sins we carry have become habits in our lives. Sometimes habits can be hard to break. They have us in a state of captivity, but God's Word comes to free us from the yoke of bondage! Yes, we can "lay aside every weight and sin" that is in our lives. Let us seek to be closer to God by reading His Word daily, delighting in the law of the Lord, not allowing it to depart from our mouths and meditating on it "day and night" to observe and to do all that is written therein (Joshua 1:8). When the Spirit of the Lord is present in our lives, we are liberated, for the scripture says, "Where the spirit of the Lord is, there is liberty" (2 Corinthians 3:17). We believe by faith that "whom the Son sets free is free indeed" (John 8:36). We can indeed become free of the yoke of bondage.

God's promises are "Yea" (Yes) and "Amen" (So be it). God's promises are confirmed. He will bring to pass the things which He has spoken for our deliverance. What a powerful privilege it is to use the scriptures in our prayers! Let us lay aside every weight and sin, resolve to *"let it all go!"* We can now run this race of salvation unencumbered! We have the promises of God to keep us encouraged. *"What are you 'weighting' for?"*

May all who read this book come to realize what a mighty arsenal we have in the Word of God and in the power of prayer. We are blessed indeed, just to know Him! And yes, we all can become more faithful in prayer! Remember to "keep on praying"!

About the Author

Dr. Mary Steele-Agee is one of fourteen children born to John and Walterene Harper Sr. She retired after thirty-two years of experience as a school teacher, principal, college professor, executive director, and school superintendent. She holds a Doctorate degree in Educational Administrator and Supervision.

Her effective leadership in the field of education has received recognition at the local, state, and national levels. This retired educator's mission is to empower others to reach their personal and professional goals. She is founder and CEO of God's JEWELS Women's Ministry. She is married to Pastor Cleveland Agee Jr., and works unselfishly beside her husband in ministry. She speaks at various women's groups, youth groups, and conferences. Dr. Steele-Agee is the mother to LaDonna and Aaron, and grandmother to Matthew, Cameron, Aaron, and Emersyn. She resides in Indiana, and firmly believes, "When God gives you a vision, He gives provisions for its successful accomplishment." To God be the glory for the things He has done!

CPSIA information can be obtained
at www.ICGtesting.com
Printed in the USA
BVHW071402170123
656441BV00002B/326